"You C___ Serious"

How to keep cool and win more in tennis...

Adrian Nicklin

ISBN: 978-1-326-22487-5

PublishNation, London

www.publishnation.co.uk

Contents

Acknowledgements

I would like to thank everybody that has supported me with my career and development so far, there are too many to mention in person.

However I would like to mention three, firstly Richard Orr, who has dedicated his time and expertise in helping the writing and completion of the book. Secondly a huge thank you to all the current and past players that have kindly given their time, experiences and their expertise, and finally a special tribute must go to the rock in life, my wife Carol, who has supported me through good and bad times, and every aspect of my life. Thank you, Carol, I love you, and I would like to dedicate this book to the newest member of our family, Katie.

Biography

My name is Adrian Nicklin. For 20 years I have worked as a tennis coach, helping players of all levels all over the UK, from the Highlands of Scotland to the hustle and bustle of London. I have also spent some time working and learning from cultures abroad, especially when working in the Middle East within The Kingdom of Bahrain. This particular opportunity allowed me to work alongside different coaches with different teaching styles and certainly helped me develop good rapport skills, as English was rarely my clients' first language.

A universally known and widely used word in the Arabian language is 'Inshallah,' meaning 'God willing' (in other words, 'it will happen when *and if* it happens'). Once I understood and started to live my life a little more by that word, I realised that tennis players are the same the world over, even though they are generally more relaxed in life than those in the UK – which we will get to.

I have worked with differing standards of tennis players, from 5-year-old children to retired, social-playing adults; from those picking up a racket for the first time, to performance players who have represented Great Britain on the world stage.

I have an Honours degree in Sports Science and hold qualifications in Neuro Linguistic Programming (NLP) and Ericksonian Hypnotherapy. This will play a significant role in the content of *You Can Be Serious*, because the enhancements I aim to make to your game have little to do with your ground strokes and backhands, and much more to do with what is known in sport as 'the top ten per cent' – in other words, your mind, and the frame of mind in which you play tennis.

Since 2007, as well as delivering tennis tuition, I have been delivering individual sessions and workshops for tennis players and clubs on mental strength training. I also deliver workshops for Tennis Scotland, training their coaches on what I call 'The Winning Edge', as well as being invited to their annual conference as a keynote speaker.

Preface – What this book is about

You Can Be Serious is written for anybody and everybody that loves to play the game of tennis, with the core purpose of helping them become a better, happier and more fulfilled player with a cool, calm and composed manner on court.

As a result, this book is written primarily for players, of any age. But, it can double as a valuable resource for coaches and parents of junior players wishing to improve a young player under their tutelage and support.

Whether you are a social club player seeking to add an extra edge, or a performance player who wants to climb to the next level, I am confident you will find the contents of *You Can Be Serious* valuable. The methods and exercises I will explain have enabled me to help hundreds of players improve their game – and in many cases enjoy more satisfaction in their life in general.

You can read this book for your own personal improvement, or it may be to help someone else with their game. However, for the purposes of consistency, I am going to address this book to you as if you are the player in question from here forward.

Through a range of concepts, techniques and drills, structured to fall in line with the routine of an everyday tennis player, *You Can Be Serious* will offer you a better understanding of how to enhance your abilities and enjoy your tennis more by improving the mental strength aspect of your game.

From exercises you can do anytime (at home, at work, on the bus), to drills you can practice on court, to specific techniques you should execute during a game, this book is designed to help you develop a mental toolkit to go out and win a match, rather than something I see far too often in the UK... going out not to lose!

Therefore, contrary to how many players operate outside the professional ranks, some of the suggestions I offer may take you out of your comfort zone a little, as I will be asking you to adopt a totally different mind-set to what may be used to.

Tennis can be as easy or as hard as you want to make it. But let's break it down to its simplest form: To win, you have to keep the ball within the white lines one more time than your opponent. That's it.

The manner in which you do this is when your game starts growing arms and legs, and you begin to implement strategies and tactics. However in turn, you may often begin to 'over complicate' how you play. This may cause your subsequent thinking to become confused as your decisions become overly complex and less rational. Thinking too much can be a bigger issue than not thinking at all in many cases.

Conversely, if you can approach your game with a clear vision and remove all the distractions, your tennis can flourish!

I believe I am good at what I teach, but I am not Harry Potter, the world-famous young wizard created in my home town of Edinburgh – I don't have a magic wand to make everything happen the way you want it to in an instant. But I do have detailed, well-practised knowledge of a number of subjects I truly believe can and will improve your tennis – and make you happier and more content as an individual. If you are willing to put in the effort and fully commit to some or all of these techniques, I will guarantee an improvement in your game, with or without the magic wand.

Within *You Can Be Serious* I am going to touch on a number of subjects, both familiar and unfamiliar. Some of them you might agree with, some you might not. Either way, however, please take time to consider every idea and suggestion openly and impartially. If in doubt, question what your tennis life means to you, where your priorities lie, and how much you want to change your tennis for the better as well as how much effort you are willing to put in to achieve your desired outcome. I trust you will come to the conclusion that it is at least worth a try.

You Can Be Serious can of course be used for 'information only' and as an interesting read – or you can throw yourself into the exercises and become an '*Always Control Emotions*' (ACE) player. The more you immerse yourself, the better the results you will experience.

I will expand more on 'ACE' as we progress – it is a pivotal concept throughout the entire book – but in short, ACE is controlling your emotional state of mind and keeping cool – regardless of what you encounter – which is easier said than done.

ACE is your mental game – and it is the next level beyond the technical skills of your physical game. There is no advice on how to hit a good forehand or effective serve-volleying in this book. Learning the bio-mechanics of tennis through quality coaching, practice and match play helps cement good habits, but learning to utilise and manage your mental state will add another dimension to your game.

By controlling your emotions you can significantly improve on the following areas of your game that, in my 20 years' experience of coaching at all levels and ages, both around the UK and abroad, I have found as the main barriers to players performing to their best. Ask yourself, "Do I suffer from one of the issues outlined below?" If so, the ideas in this book are a must to allow you to play to your best.

- Does your confidence or trust in yourself disappear during matches?
- Do you find it difficult to hold your concentration during a match?
- Has your love of playing the game been reduced or disappeared?

- Do you give away too many points when you have a supposedly 'easy' shot?
- Are you losing too many close matches?
- Do you miss the same shots time and again and don't know how to fix it on the spot?
- Do you lose to players you are convinced you should be beating on a regular basis?
- Do you play great in practice, but play badly in the heat of a competitive match?
- Do you get distracted by thinking about other things when playing, or by who is watching you?

I would be very surprised if at least a couple of the sentences above did not resonate with you. Even the finest players in the world suffer from some of these issues from time to time – quite publically in some cases.

Everybody has their favourite tennis player. From the heroes of modern era – Federer, Williams, Murray, Nadal, Djokovic, Sharapova and Laura Robson, to the legends of the past – Sampras, Graf, Agassi, King, Navratilova, McEnroe, Becker and Borg, the list is endless.

Past and present, each have their own unique style, each play the game with different tactical, technical and physical preferences and skill sets. But what they all possess, to have allowed them to reach the pinnacle of the game, is mental toughness. This is arguably the main reason behind the success, and making of, these champions – and indeed the top men and women in any sport.

Mental training works in sport, and it works especially well in tennis – it is the loneliest of sports, so strength of character and a solid temperament are crucial weapons in the successful player's armoury. The mind controls the body, not the other way round, so most problems in tennis are simply due to the mind being untrained to perform correctly. A properly trained mind allows a player to master their game and play to their best.

After years of teaching and observing, it became very obvious to me that there was a direct correlation between heightened emotional stress levels and diminishing performance – not just in tennis but other sports too, as well as general life experiences. This may not be an earth shattering statement, but it is certainly something we can all appreciate – and most would just accept this as a fact of life. But I refuse to accept it. I believe we can train our brain for improvement in the same way we can train any other muscle in our body.

When I talk to my clients regarding their own tennis game, they nearly always attribute their issues on court to bad technique or not being fit enough. Unfortunately, although these areas can always be improved, often the main reason for a poor performance was what was going on in their head. Henceforth, I realised that focusing on improving this side of their game significantly enhanced their performance.

There are a number of books, courses and websites out there that address the theory of mental strength training. I have personally observed and absorbed what many of them have to offer and all have their own merits.

So what I am offering to you in *You Can Be Serious* is my unique personal account of what works for my clients – tried and tested time and again over many years. You may be hearing my name for the first time, and I have yet to coach a top player to Grand Slam success. But I do possess proven, relevant, practical methods to make a difference right here, right now, to you as a tennis player and as a person.

This is my way, and I have enjoyed consistently positive results and feedback. *You Can Be Serious* is therefore designed to feel like the coaching sessions I deliver to my clients – relaxed but revitalising, informal but informative.

To keep this promise, you will find that *You Can Be Serious* will:

- <u>Be broken down into specific areas</u>: The concepts are laid out in a suggested order of implementation, but you will just as easily be able to dip in and out of each chapter and concept as you please – just as you would decide to work on your backhand or your serve on any given day, depending on your own need.

- <u>Keep you in control</u>: *You Can Be Serious* is at its core a coaching manual. But it is also a light, stress-free, easy read, with anecdotes and observations that any tennis fan will appreciate. So digest the information and try out the techniques in your own time at your own pace.

- <u>Give you practical advice</u>: There are dozens of on and off court exercises – ones you can do as you read, ones you will sit down and focus on at home, and others you can take into a game.

- <u>Be backed up by the best</u>: It's all very well telling you about the techniques I use with everyday players, every day. But to show you how effective they are, *You Can Be Serious* will also give you direct examples from the professionals. In some cases this may be observations of the top players in action, while at other points you will read insights from professional, international players interviewed exclusively for *You Can Be Serious*.

Finally, the methods and exercises are laid out in a logical order – in <u>accordance with how you would prepare for a tennis match</u>. So at various points I will highlight that a certain technique is best practised in the days leading up to a game, in preparation on the day of a game, during a game or after.

I wish you every success in tennis – and trust that *You Can Be Serious* will help you find it.

Introduction

We live in a stressful world of instants. Everyone wants everything done – yesterday. The world moves at breakneck speed, and everyone occupying it seems to be dashing around in a swirl of frenetic but ill-directed energy.

Plus, we stress. Boy, do we stress. And it is happening more often – there was a 7% increase in stress-related admissions to hospitals in 2014 alone in England. It is one of the biggest yet most unacknowledged issues that Western human beings deal with today. We worry about money, which causes us to worry about work, which takes us back to worrying about money again. At work we are stressed about our next appraisal, panicking about that big presentation, concerned that the weather will stop us from getting our job done. We get stressed by too much work, and even more so when there isn't enough. Often, that stress unravels into our personal lives too.

We stress about our friends and relatives. They are too old, too fat, too poor or too lazy. Our children are often stressed with exams or relationships. As parents, we spend too much time stressing about our children – worrying that they are spending more and more time engaged in screen based activity – watching TV, playing games consoles and gossiping on social networking sites – and not enough time getting fit and healthy.

We complain if a parcel arrives one day late or if the phone call we expected at 3pm didn't come. If the queue at the checkout is too long we get impatient. Often, we go online and complain to others!

In short, we've got a problem with stress. So, wouldn't it be nice to switch off and be stress free, just for an hour or two? To have fun and forget about the maelstrom of worry that surrounds us?

That's what sport is all about. It's why many – indeed most – of us do it. Sure, we like to win, we love to see ourselves improve and it's good to stay fit. But isn't the best bit just being able to forget the rigours of daily life and focus on something more basic – like hitting a fuzzy yellow ball with a lattice of strings tightly stitched onto a fibreglass stick?

Yet, far too frequently, sport – and in our case, tennis – can simply become an extra line on the list of things that stress us out. We worry that we will play poorly, or mope around when our fears become reality. "I'm supposed to enjoy this!" (We silently scream to ourselves.) So, in a world flowing over with stress, it would be welcome respite to be able to fully enjoy your tennis, and switch off from life for an hour or two, wouldn't it? Or, even better, wouldn't it be wonderful to reduce the stress levels of life in general?

Many times in my tennis coaching career I have witnessed clients rushing in from their busy life for a tennis lesson, or a tennis match. They normally bring all the baggage of what is happening in their life onto the court and subsequently do not have as good and productive a lesson or match as they could have had.

Over time, I realised that if my clients arrived on court having left all that baggage at the door, or they had techniques to help themselves enjoy a fun, stress free lesson, they achieved significantly improved results. In turn, this created a sense of accomplishment and enjoyment from their session – which is why 99% of players actually step onto the court in the first place. So they leave happier than when they arrived, feeling emotionally fulfilled.

What the latter group have in common with each other is a clarity of purpose. They know why they choose to play tennis and what they enjoy about it, and focus on achieving those simple goals. Their motivation is crystal clear and at the forefront of their minds.

So the first thing we will do in this book is pin down exactly what it is you want from your tennis, and work from there. You've probably never thought about it like that before, but it makes sense, doesn't it? *Focusing on what you want*. After all, when you are hungry and need to satisfy that hunger, you go straight to the fridge or the café, don't you? You don't (or at least, you shouldn't) decide at that very moment to do the vacuuming, wash the car and lodge a cheque at the bank, do you?

Remember, the vast majority of us (unfortunately) don't (or can't) play for financial gain, so there has to be another trigger for lacing up those tennis shoes and spending a fortune on tubes of balls. And if you can find your true, personal motivation for picking up a racket, and focus on that, you can start to strip away all the distractions of life and begin playing to your best!

I have found that most people who play amateur sport don't actually want 'coached' for the express purpose of winning. Playing purely to win is what the professionals do. Yes, it is desirable, and we certainly dislike losing, but it's not the reason most people step into the competitive arena in the first place. More often, winning is a welcome by-product that comes from our love of the sport we play.

What we actually want is our emotional needs, desires, dreams and goals fulfilled. Players want a good serve or forehand for more than the sake of having one and telling their friends. They want it because they have an emotional need for to achieve an outcome that has personal significance and is important to them. The more you can understand what your emotional needs, desires or goals are, the more you can help yourself move towards them. So let's look at what those hopes and dreams are...

Section 1 – Getting Personal

As I will mention often in this book, as a coach I tend to focus more on the *person* in front of me, rather than the *player*. Each individual is the driving force behind their own tennis game, and more often than not it is their mood, outlook and character that has the big impact on their performance – be that positive or negative – rather than their ability.

So before you start blaming your forehand or your fitness for your latest slump in form, have a think about the kind of person, and player, you are...

Why do I play Tennis?

This may seem an obvious, almost pedantic question. But take a moment to seriously consider it. Think about the days and hours building up to the moment you take to court. Are you looking forward to it? What do you picture yourself doing in your head?

A lot of people think the reason they play tennis, or any sport that matter, is to 'win'. Everyone loves winning. But when you think ahead to the next time you play, is it yourself celebrating that you see? Or is it yourself moving freely around the court, hitting good shots, having fun with your friends or teammates?

So ask yourself again, why do you play? Is it to win? Or is it something else?

Exercise 1 – The Acid Test

Take a minute and list your top 5 reasons for playing tennis, ranking them in order of importance. Some examples may be: For fun; to enhance fitness; to improve; to win; to socialise; to achieve something; for distraction / leisure.

1.	Fun
2.	compete
3.	social
4.	fitness
5.	coordination

Happy with your reasoning? Sure? OK, let's move on...

Now from these five areas ask yourself, "In the longer term, am I completely fulfilling all these areas?"
If so, maybe you don't need this book. But keep reading just in case you're fooling yourself. However if you answer, "No" or "Probably not", then ask yourself two questions:

- "If not, why not?"
- "What can I do about it?"

This is where the *You Can Be Serious* really starts. Because, regardless of how good or bad you believe you are at tennis, as players of the game we all have one thing in common: *we want to have a fulfilling experience*. Therefore, whatever you're reasons for playing, at their heart they should offer you one thing: Fulfilment.

Your player profile

Now that you have established *why* you play, let's consider *how* you play. Do you know what kind of player you are? What are your strengths and weaknesses? What worries your opponents when they play you, and where do they try to get the better of you? Are you a physical player or a crafty player? Are you Mrs Calm or Mr Angry?

Well, let's start by focusing on the positives. Recognising the areas of your game that are good, rather than always looking at what is letting you down, is the first, basic step in giving you a solid foundation of trust and confidence in your own ability to go out and fulfil your tennis ambitions.

Also, of course, it is important to acknowledge areas of your game that need to be improved, but, be sure to give yourself a pat on your back for the aspects of your game you feel are strong. These areas will form the core of your 'player profile' when deciding what type of tennis player you are and what sort of game plan will suit you!

The exercise below is a great one for a junior player trying to find a style that suits them. I have even used this same technique for working with students in the context of music and even studying for exams. So take a few moments to profile your game and answer the following four questions as truthfully as possible – you can write the answers down if you feel this may help:

- What is my best and most proud tennis achievement to date?

- What is my ideal, realistic goal as a tennis player?

- As a tennis player what do I feel are my main weapons on court? (List a top 5 from areas including technical, tactical, physical or mental ability.)

- What are the five areas of your game you feel you need to improve on? (Think about where you often lose points and even matches.)

Now, having answered these questions and scrutinised your game, I trust that, even though you are still the same player you were yesterday, you now have a slightly 'warmer' feeling about your game. You realise what you have to offer as a player – to a team or to yourself.

And, having thought about your weaknesses, you also should now have a fairly clear idea about how you can get even better, if you are willing to put the work in.

However, you may still feel a lack of confidence. This is fine, and is probably down to a lack of true trust in your own ability. You know your strengths but are aware that they don't always stand up to stern testing. And though you know your weaknesses and try to avoid them, it is difficult to stop them from creeping into your game, especially when an opponent is putting you under pressure. That is fine for now – we will look at addressing this.

To fully allow yourself to play with trust you must know when and why your trust breaks down. This can be a very fragile psychological part of your game. But now that you have deconstructed it, we can begin to rebuild, adding and enhancing along the way with the help of the biggest weapon in every player's arsenal: The mind...

NLP – An introduction

NLP (Neuro Linguistic Programming) has influenced my learning, my teaching and coaching, and to large extent it has shaped the content of this book. I have broken down what it means in the paragraphs below, but in essence NLP is being able to understand and adapt what we say and what we do to our own benefit – I'm sure you'll agree that sounds a lot more straightforward than the name 'Neuro Linguistic Programming' suggests!

As a result I will ask you to apply some of the principles of NLP on occasion, but this will only be basic, entry-level NLP. If you find you are curious to know more about NLP having given it a go, there are countless books and courses available across the UK.

NLP was created in the 1970's by Richard Bandler, a mathematician, and John Grinder, a linguistic professor. In simple terms, my definition of Neuro-Linguistic Programming is the 'copying of excellence' by learning how to monitor and adapt your thinking to gain the best results possible for yourself. NLP uses both conscious and unconscious mental processes that lead to increased communication skills, confidence, motivation and success, and is directly related to increasing your ability to influence and persuade. It is also effective in overcoming blocks or barriers caused by a lack of these skills. The full description is:

NEURO   Refers to how the mind and body interact, by becoming aware of how we think. Literally meaning 'nerve' or 'nervous system', it implies we can influence our outcomes from the inside out.

LINGUISTIC   Refers to the insight into a person's thinking and how we use language, both internal and external, verbal and nonverbal. By paying mindful attention to our language we can shift our thinking and master our communication skills.

PROGRAMMING   Refers to the study of the thinking and behavioural patterns or strategies which people use in their daily lives. By acquiring an understanding of these strategies we can change them, keep them or improve on them to increase our potential.

NLP can and is being used in all areas of work and life: sales, marketing, teaching, counselling, HR, personal development, and of course in sport. The difference it makes at all levels is significant, and sport demonstrates this vividly.

For example, until recently, in both amateur and high-level sport the athlete or team that were a little fitter, had more desire or had more time to practice tended to come out on top. In a tight match, those small percentages made a difference, much more so than ability.

However now, in top-tier sport, those days are a distant memory. It is extremely difficult to win over an opponent through physicality and ability alone. In the modern professional era, athletes are all as fit as each other, train full time and have all the support necessary to technically and physically excel. But the body can only be pushed so far, so very often there has to be something else that makes that 1% different between winning a gold medal and not even getting into the final. That difference is what goes on inside your head, that inner game. It is your 'inner-game' we are going to look at in this book. But first, let's have a quick look at what had a major impact on mine. And it probably isn't what you think...

Don't Look Back In Anger!

Before we explore my experiences and exercises relating to the game of tennis, I would like to share a little bit about my past, to give you an understanding of who I am, where I have come from and why I believe so strongly in the power of the mind. This story has nothing and everything to do with tennis.

It has helped to shape who I am today, and is the core reason behind why I truly believe in the power of the inner game, for helping with tennis – my own game and that of others – and also life in general.

I am about to recall an incident which led to the worst period of my life. I am not telling this story for sympathy, or because I think I deserve your admiration. A lot of people have had and will have stories to tell that are much more harrowing. I simply hope this gives you some context as to why I believe so strongly in the power of the mind.

This chapter of my life goes back to the spring of 1997, back when Tony Blair had yet to become Prime Minister, Oasis were the biggest band in Britain, and mobiles were used for making phone calls. I had graduated from university the previous summer, and I didn't have a clear idea about what I wanted to do or where my life was going to take me.

There was one thing I was sure of though – I was done with studying for a while and decided to take a year out, moving back home to live with my parents in central Scotland.

I started working full time in a large hotel leisure complex as a fitness instructor, lifeguard and tennis coach. It was never my intention for this to turn into my long term vocation.

The distance from the hotel to my home was just over a mile as the crow flies, so I usually chose to walk to and from work if the weather allowed. My usual route took me through an area which had tall three-storey tenement blocks on the left hand side and large Victorian houses on the opposite side, before entering a small parkland area. I lived on the other side of the park in a newly built estate.

As you can imagine from the description, this twice-daily journey was usually pretty uneventful. I'm sure most of you will partake in similar journeys on a regular basis – almost on autopilot. The concept of anything unusual happening is not even in your mind – it is routine, unchanging and indistinguishable from one day to the next.

So as I headed home on this night around 11pm, it was just another evening after another day at work. The weather was clear and a bit chilly for spring, with not a soul about. Yet for some reason on this night, I don't know why, but I turned around to look behind. As I did, I focussed on three figures about 200 metres away, running in my direction. However, naively perhaps, I turned back and continued walking down the road, feeling a bit wary but not too alarmed as I had done nothing to aggravate any situation.

Then I heard them closing in on me. I turned round again and I saw it was three lads, in their late teens, obviously under the influence of drink or drugs, or both. Now I was beginning to get a little alarmed, but I kept walking.

They edged closer and closer until it became obvious I was the focus of their attention. And then they were upon me. I turned and faced them. One of the boys stayed in front of me while the remaining two moved round behind my back.

One of the boys in front of me shouted in my face and pushed me. I pushed him back, but as did I was hit on the back of my skull by one of the boys. I fell like a stone to the ground, straight onto the road.

From that point onwards, it is only eye witness reports that piece what happened next together. The road itself was deserted - no cars, no other walkers. Only two people hiding behind their curtains in one of the nearby houses saw what was happening. Thankfully they called for the police and an ambulance whilst watching helplessly.

I lay there unconscious for a full five minutes while the three boys used my head as a football. There was no sense of control in what they were doing – they were unforgiving and ferocious, with no thought of the consequences for me or for themselves.

I am not trying to shock anybody but this is the stark and brutal reality of what goes on in our streets most weeks in most towns in Britain. I was just the unlucky one that night.

The three boys left me when they heard the sirens approaching. When the paramedics arrived I wasn't breathing. They started CPR on me, and rushed me to the nearest casualty unit about 20 miles away.

Now, believe it or not, in some ways I was lucky. If this had happened 200 metres further down the road, it might have been the end for me, as I would have been attacked in the park with nobody watching. But because it happened on that street I am here to tell the tale and enjoy my life.

I woke up in casualty, with tubes coming out of me all over. My Mum and Dad were sitting next to me, my sister was outside the room, and my brother was driving 160 miles to be by my side. Nobody knew whether I would be brain damaged until I regained consciousness. I can only imagine how tortured they felt.

Thankfully, the physical scars and bruises healed quickly and well. I had my teeth repaired and was told my memory would not heal completely but would improve over time, all of which did and has happened. But the external damage was just one aspect of my recovery. In many ways, it was the easiest. Outwardly everything went back to normal over a period of time. However, internally, I was a mess.

After several weeks I stepped back onto the tennis court. I was bored and wanted to hit a ball again. But when the ball was played to me I just fell over. My body was not ready because my brain could not concentrate on hitting the ball and move my body towards it at the same time. It could manage one or the other, but not both.

I spent a further two months at home building up my strength. I then decided to leave my home town (just to escape the area), and I took up a kind offer from a couple of close university friends.

First, I took some work in Kent, helping with summer tennis camps for kids. Then I bunked up with another friend in the bright lights of London – he had just started working with the Metropolitan Police and had bought his first flat.

I spent a few months in London. But I couldn't (or wouldn't) find a job, instead choosing to sign on the dole and mope around. Eventually I did find a job as a lifeguard in a public swimming pool, but I was becoming more and more withdrawn, I could feel it. It was like a downward spiral taking me to places I didn't want to go.

I gave up and moved back home as I needed help. I had lost all sense of emotion. I couldn't laugh, I couldn't cry, I just had nothing. My Dad was concerned that I was becoming suicidal. To be honest, looking back, I didn't know what was going on or where I was going to end up.

I started a course of counselling that lasted about four months, twice-weekly – and it was a revelation. It wasn't like I had imagined it, as you see it on TV – on a couch in a small room, uncomfortable silences, sitting opposite a stranger. In this case it was my retired deputy head from school.

"Tell me what you are feeling," she asked.

"Nothing," I replied.

Then we sat some more. She didn't say anything. I certainly didn't say anything. Over the next two months I started to open up just a little, and then a little more until, despite the fact I still couldn't remember what had happened to me, I could talk about it. About the consequences of the incidents, the boys, the trial (which I will not go into, suffice to say I do not have a lot of faith in our justice system and probably never will).

After about four months I started looking forward to our chats. And then one day something happened – one of those moments in your life when you feel something has shifted.

We were talking, really talking, about a whole range of issues. I could feel my eyes welling up with tears. I couldn't stop it, she took my hand and I cried and all of a sudden I felt all my emotions coming back.

We only had one more session after that one. I was beginning to be in touch with my emotions again. I embarked on a number of self-help books and systems to help me gain control of my life.

This experience started me on the path to realising the complexity of the human mind – its powers and its weaknesses – and I wanted to know more. This is when I first came into contact with NLP and I realised I had more of a choice in my life than I ever imagined.

Prior to my accident, I had studied sports psychology at university. I thought I knew the power of the mind, especially within a sporting context. But I quickly realised how naïve I had been – I had no comprehension of the bigger picture. This event in my life changed everything for me – my entire outlook. It pushed me towards learning and finding out more and more about the mind and what a remarkable, complex, but also fragile and sensitive machine it can be.

It is very easy to look back or live in a particular moment and feel sorry for ourselves, to blame a list of circumstances as to why things have gone wrong. But I believe everybody has good and bad luck in their lives, and it is how we deal with these situations, however challenging, that makes the difference in how successful and fulfilling your life becomes.

Only from coming out the other side of that awful period in my life do I feel truly lucky with life and what it has to throw up. I now take a positive outlook on everything.

I called this chapter 'don't look back in anger' because, for all of us, there will be moments in your life when you experience tough times. But you have to be resilient, push through and fight for what you want, whether it is for your health, career, family, or indeed your tennis, as often it is all too easy to give up. We all need to overcome our demons become stronger competitors. I will mention it often, but there is no better example than Andy Murray, and how he slowly but surely grew into a Wimbledon winner.

I have been brutally frank and honest with you about my experience. The outcome of it is that I have become much more aware of and in touch with my own mind. I am constantly conscious of my own 'inner game'. That 'inner game' that we all hear, that 'inner game' that more often than not is giving us negative thoughts. We all have the ability to turn this round to our benefit.

In the next few chapters I will work my way through a number of experiences and exercises to allow *your* mind to explore what I feel are the core areas to helping understand and adapt to suit your needs.

This will of course be for the development of your tennis game, but it can be taken and applied for personal development in your life as a whole. Tennis is just a part of the bigger picture, but either way it will make you a more rounded, happier person. That has got to be worth a go!

Section 2 – The Theory

Now that we have established who you are as a tennis player, we can begin to get down to business. But, just as in business, it is foolish to rush into an investment or deal without doing your due diligence and background research. And so we must take the same, professional, conscientious approach to improving our tennis. So this section establishes a solid base by looking at the central ideals of what we are aiming to achieve.

The objective of *You Can Be Serious* is to help build you into a better, happier tennis player – but in order to achieve that, we must first take a look at the blueprint and lay the foundations...

Always Control Emotions (ACE)

Let's get to the root of things. To be successful in tennis, you've got to be mentally tough. If you need convincing, look no further than Britain's very own Andy Murray. How many gut-wrenching grand slam final losses did the Scot have to endure before he finally claimed Olympic Gold and the US Open Final in a few glorious weeks back in 2012, topped off with the Wimbledon championship in July 2013? (The answer is four – two Australian Open Finals, one US Open Final and one Wimbledon Final from 2008-12.)

Most, or certainly many people, would allow such monumental disappointment, and indeed such all-engulfing pressure in terms of Wimbledon, to overwhelm them –

causing them to give up altogether. But Murray continued to push for the breakthrough and win those titles.

And even the most casual of tennis fans will have been aware Murray's progression over those years. In literal terms, he transformed from boy to man. But there was an altogether deeper change, in his spirit and his mind-set as well as his body that was clear to see. His ability was never in doubt. He is an exceptional tennis player. But look back at how Murray developed, particularly from 2008 (his first Grand Slam final, the US Open) to 2012, and you will see they are two completely different people in terms of their inner belief, even if his steadfast will remained the same.

In 2008 Murray was, in relative terms, still quite 'lean' for an elite athlete. For a normal 21-year-old, he was certainly extremely fit. But compared to his contemporaries – Rafael Nadal and Novak Djokovic – he lacked physical presence. So in his off-seasons Murray sacrificed Christmas at home and spent the winter months in Miami adding pounds of muscle to his frame and improving his stamina.

That strength and fitness is evident in the Andy Murray we see today. But even more obvious is the new, considered, controlled, calm Murray. Remember the outbursts, the swearing, and the shouting? It was plain to see Andy was letting his own mind get the better of him in his early years.

Now, he has the mental strength and composure to back up his physical ability.

Of course, Andy Murray has his own team of world class coaches, psychologists and advisors. So I can't tell you what he specifically did. But I feel pretty confident that a version of what I call the "*ACE* approach", standing for "*A*lways *C*ontrol *E*motions", is part of the present-day Murray prototype's make-up.

Imagine his emotions as he allowed three match-points to slip away in that Wimbledon final. I'm sure you, if you were watching, felt much like I did – your heart was pounding, your forehead sweating, unable to contain your mix of anxiety and excitement. No doubt you and I both did our fair share of shouting at the TV that hot Sunday afternoon.

You also probably thought, as I did, that he had blown his chance when Djokovic pulled the match back to deuce, and then had three break points of his own to regain the initiative. But imagine how Murray felt! And, even more so, consider how impressively he controlled his emotions to close out the game, set, match and championship for the first time in 77 years.

Andy did it. He did it for himself but it felt like the greatest of victories for all of us. But now, think back again to the player he once was several years before. Quite a change, isn't it? He was a picture of serenity compared to his earlier days – in complete control at all times.

Murray (now) understands that emotions dictate our mental state, and the calmer we are the easier it is to think rationally, in life or on a tennis court. Obvious but true. How often have you seen (whether it was you or someone else) an individual lose their temper with a child, partner or colleague, only to admit later that it was probably the worst way to deal with the situation?

In the context of why I am writing this book, and of course, Andy Murray, the calmer we are, the better decisions we make, leading to a better performance and results, which in turn ultimately leads to a more enjoyable experience of the game of tennis. Murray certainly enjoyed the minutes and days that followed his win at Wimbledon.

Often people will say to me that they are angry, they are sad, they are disappointed, they are nervous. But what they really mean to say is they are *feeling* angry, *feeling* sad, *feeling* disappointed or *feeling* nervous.

By acknowledging that anger or sadness (or frustration or impatience) is a feeling, rather than a permanent state of mind, it allows these people to take responsibility and control of their emotions. They are generally not angry or sad people by default. They are normal people suffering from a fleeting moment of negative emotion.

Anyone can change how they feel in an instant. Take a moment to close your eyes and think about something or someone in your life that makes you happy. Or imagine you have won the lottery and you are thinking how to spend the money: new house (with a gym and a pool and a home cinema!); giving up work; holidays and holiday homes; cars and gadgets; giving money and gifts to family, friends and charity. This thought makes you *feel* happy. It doesn't make you a happy person (and even if you did win, remember money doesn't buy happiness!), but you can savour the emotion for a moment.

Stay with this feeling for a few moments longer. Paint a picture of it in your head. See, hear and really feel all the emotions, colours, faces and noises (and cars and palm trees and cocktails), and enjoy the experience.

When you bring yourself back to reality, your life is the same as it was one minute ago. But do you feel a little happier?

Now close your eyes again and think about someone or something that really annoys or upsets you. Again, bring the experience to life, reconstruct it like an episode of *Crime watch*. You can imagine what I think about when I go to this place.

Stay with it for a moment, but not for too long. Your mood has changed for the worse, hasn't it? That example shows how fickle emotions can be. You chose to control your mood. Within a few seconds you have experienced two contrasting emotions and neither were down to chance. Both of them you chose to experience, both you decided to change.

It is normally life experience that determines and influences your own responses and what emotions are subsequently felt by you. But, as you have seen, you can choose to control your own emotions instead. This is obviously not a technique I would advise to help you climb out of more profoundly difficult, genuinely life-affecting circumstances, but tennis is *just a game*.

Here, we are simply talking about the moment you hit a ball a few centimetres further to the left or right than you intended, and how to deal with it emotionally. No big deal at all, except for that ill-placed white line which means you have lost a point, rather than gained one. Let's take a more detailed look….

Imagine that point is an important point. You are serving 4-5 down at 30-40 in the deciding set, knowing if you lose this point, you have lost the match. You also know that if you win it, you're back in the game with a chance of coming back. It's still just a single point, but this can obviously bring a different emotional response than if you are in the first point of the first game.

How would you feel at that moment? Would you be like Andy Murray on championship point, calm and focused? Or would you be like I was on the couch watching Murray, sweaty and pulsating with nerves?

How would you be feeling if your opponent had already broken your serve several times in this game? And, even worse, at 30-30 you double-faulted, literally handing your opponent a match-point. Would that affect your emotions, your confidence at this point?

Now imagine you had 15,000 spectators, 20 million television viewers (in the UK alone) and 77 years of expectation on your shoulders. OK, maybe that's a step too far, but ask yourself, what impact does an audience have on your tennis? When you are playing with no one watching your match, does this bring a different emotional response from you than if 20 people are watching? Would it make any difference to how you felt as you tossed the ball up to serve?

I know in my club that some players can't even bear to have a person talking near the court, they are so easily distracted.

OK that's enough. Quite possibly you are stressed just imagining this scenario, let alone playing it out. Therefore when we are *feeling* angry, frustrated or anxious on court, we expend more emotional energy and our thinking and decision making is likely to be disrupted. This leads to picking the wrong option on court or not concentrating fully on our shot, leading to a poorer performance and results. It also brings on what is commonly known in the game as choking, when stress makes it harder to coordinate our muscles!

So, the big question: *How do we avoid these issues?*

Let's consider a different situation. Imagine two young tennis players of similar ability make it to Wimbledon for the first time, and they are drawn against each other in the opening round. It's obviously a huge moment for them – the moment they can genuinely say to themselves they are a top player, playing in the world's biggest and most historic tennis tournament. Each of the individuals may well imagine different and contrasting things as the match approaches.

One of the players could be nervous about how well she will play, and is worried about making mistakes and looking silly on TV. She worries she will be unable to play well in such a big match. She feels it before she even steps on court. Her muscles are tense and she is anxious. This player is likely to feel exposed and uncertain and her performance will be poor – visibly so. Her movement will be clunky and she will strike the ball tentatively. Her physical play is reflecting her emotional state – apprehensive and uncomfortable. Each poor shot emits a shriek of frustration and her heart sinks point by point.

The other player, conversely, might imagine her first appearance at Wimbledon as the experience of a lifetime. For her, this is like a child's first trip to Disneyland – her ultimate dream fulfilled and she can't wait. She fully intends to go out and enjoy the moment and can't wait to get onto those pristine, lush green courts in front of the world-famous Wimbledon crowds. She feels liberated and relaxed and her play is likely to reflect these emotions – striking the ball cleanly and moving fluidly. "She looks like a natural", the commentators may purr.

As you can see, one player is evidently 'choking', while the other is simply enjoying her opportunity. But aren't they both facing the exact same scenario? Why is it that the same event evokes two different responses, in turn leading to two very different performances?

Then take the example of Gordon Reid. Gordon is Britain's top wheelchair tennis player. By the age of 21, he had already competed at two Paralympic Games (Beijing 2008 and London 2012, where he reached the quarter final) and holds a singles ranking of 6th in the world and a doubles world ranking of 4th.

The rules of wheelchair tennis are identical to able-bodied tennis, except that the ball is allowed to bounce twice before a player must strike it. Competing at the thick end of most major championships around the world, Gordon is more aware than most of the significance of mental strength.

"It's very important," he states. "It's a massive part of all sports, but tennis especially is well known as being very mentally demanding. Having started playing internationally so young, I had to learn how important it is very quickly, and adapt to be on a par with the top players in the world. The more you play against those players, the clearer it becomes. So preparing myself mentally has become a big part of my training.

On the other end of the age spectrum, Reid uses the example of his Austrian counterpart, Martin Legner, as to why mental strength can often be the difference between winning and losing.

"Martin is 51 years-old and has been on the [NEC Wheelchair Tennis] Tour for 30 years. He plays about 20 tournaments a year and is still in the world's top 20. He will regularly come up against players who are much younger and therefore fitter, faster and stronger than him. But he can read the game so well, he can just grind the points out, moving players round the court and picking on their weaknesses until they self-combust. He beats players mentally."

So how do you ensure that next time you step on court, you are the player brimming with confidence, ready to perform? How do you enable yourself to play that match-saving point with freedom and composure? How can you ensure that you *Always Control Emotions*?

Programming your mind to change your interpretation of a situation is the first step in helping you learn how to manage your emotions. When you can manage your emotions, you can perform to your best. And when you hit that serve – you guessed it – it will be ACE.

Programme Your Mind

At any given time in a match you are either thinking about your game in a positive, assured way or thinking in a way that causes self-doubt to creep in and affect your confidence in a negative way. There are thousands of thoughts and emotions that run through your mind during a tennis match and these have a huge effect upon your match results on court.

So your job is to ensure that your mind is working for you, rather than against you. Any player can dramatically improve their results using this simple form of mental strength training. And it begins by talking yourself up.

A human thinks approximately 60,000 thoughts a day, and being on court does not interrupt its progress. You are talking to yourself constantly on court. So, by programming your mind *positively* with powerful words, images and emotions, you will get vastly improved results. Sound too obvious? Consider what the experts say...

Lauren Robins, (MS, LMT) writes in *The Indefinite Body*: "Thoughts create chemicals that pour into the rivers and streams coursing through our body. Within 20 seconds, the chemical composition of the body is altered by a thought, having an acid or alkaline effect... As we persevere on limiting, negative thoughts, our nervous system sends chemicals to muscles; our physical body contracts and thinking becomes foggy."

Cathy Chapman, (PhD, LCSW), a licensed clinical social worker writes in *Strengthening the Immune System*: "If you are someone who thinks sad, angry or negative thoughts most of the day, you are weakening your immune system. The chemicals in your body which fight off infection can be *clinically shown* to decrease."

Dr. Joseph Dispenza in *Physics, the Brain and Your Reality* says: "The thinking brain, the neo cortex, is the seed of our freewill and allows us to have a choice and opinion. The one thing I noticed about people who had changes in health [is that they] had changed their thinking too. If they changed their thinking, was the effect in the brain sending a new signal to their body? The answer is yes... Our thoughts have a direct connection to our direct level of health. Thoughts make a chemical. If you have happy thoughts then you're producing chemicals that make you feel happy. It you have negative thoughts, angry thoughts or insecure thoughts, those thoughts make chemicals to make you feel how you're thinking… There is sound evidence that our thoughts do matter. We always replace those old patterns with a greater ideal of ourselves. If rehearsed mentally, we will grow new circuits in the brain, the platform on which we stand to execute a new level of self."

And Dr Joseph M Carver (PhD), in the article *Emotional Memory Management: Positive Control over Your Memory* observes: "Thoughts change brain chemistry. That sounds so simple but that's the way it is, with our thoughts changing neurotransmitters on a daily basis. If a man walks into a room with a gun, we think "threat", and the brain releases norepinephrine. We become tense, alert, develop sweaty palms, and our heart beats faster. If he then bites the barrel of the gun, telling us the gun is actually chocolate, the brain rapidly changes its opinion and we relax and laugh — the joke is on us… We feel what we think!

"Positive thinking works. As the above example suggests, what we think about a situation actually creates our mood. Passed over for a promotion, we can either think we'll never get ahead in this job (lowering serotonin and making us depressed) or assume that we are being held back for another promotion or job transfer (makes a better mood)."

Those were four entirely different world experts on the human mind making the same compelling point: The way you think has a direct impact on how you behave. Therefore *controlling your thoughts during a tennis match may help you to transform your results*. It's all about the power of positive thinking.

Need more convincing? Look no further than the sports psychologist Alexis Castorri, who worked with both Andy Murray and Ivan Lendl, the legendary player and coach that took Murray to Olympic and Grand Slam success.

Castorri said in an interview with *The Tennis Space*: "The mind and body work together, so devising a system that progressively relaxes and then sharpens the focus in preparation for competing [is very important]. For each person this is different, the point being develop one that works for you and then stick to it."

Even the few words you say out loud to yourself during a match have a major effect. Telling yourself 'good shot, keep it up' every time you win a point will keep your positive mindset ticking over. Or patting yourself on the back after a good shot by saying a simple 'Yes' or 'Come on'. We will get to this in more detail in subsequent chapters (remember, we're still on the theory).

Just watch the pros and your will get the picture. Every time Serena Williams or Rafael Nadal plays a winning shot, they congratulate themselves before shifting their focus to the next point. NBA basketballers and NFL footballers take this to another level in the US with over the top celebrations – it consolidates a positive moment. That's because it is the *quality* of these thoughts which makes the difference.

Conversely, it is now well known that negative thoughts lead to problems such as fear, extreme nervousness, and intimidation, lack of belief, worry, silly mistakes, anger, and frustration. Thinking negative thoughts during a match and you will get a negative result. So what do you do? You do what all the world's top players do – you accept that negativity, unforced errors, poor form and indeed plain old bad luck will creep into your game – but you strive to avoid it by seeking out and maintaining you're 'Ideal Performance State'.

The 'Ideal Performance State' for Tennis

Many club players and even juniors have sufficient mental strength to keep rallies going until their opponent makes a mistake, or play with enough discipline to see out a close game. Equally though, most of us will have lost against opponents we are sure were inferior, or at least more likely to lose than we were. I am sure we have all played matches against the notorious 'hacker', the player that 'moon balls' his returns and tries to frustrate you.

Very often this player will win because you become frustrated with their clumsy style, and you end up thinking more about how they are playing than your own game. As a result you lose your emotional control, and the game, by not managing *your own* match play, *your own* shot production and *your own* patterns of play.

It seems obvious, but players of all ages and abilities should take responsibility for their own tennis. When you step on to a court you must have true confidence which will make you go out and play to *win* a match, rather than *not lose it*.

When you play a match, it could be against another club or team, a box league or ladder match, your own club championship, or even a friendly match that means nothing to anybody else but the two or four of you playing (though it still might be somebody you really want to beat). And because it is important to you, this might cause a feeling of tension, anxiety or a lack of confidence and concentration – so before the game has even started you are mentally out of sorts.

Next, the annoying replay in your mind of your last poor shot, or the lack of ability to control your emotional state will affect your body and subsequently your level of performance. It may even turn out to be something not related to your game that is affecting your mind-set. A bad day at work or school, your partner, what you are having for dinner ('did I remember to defrost the chicken?'); anything can detract your focus away from play.

So you can see why some days you can win a match 6-4, 6-2 but a few days later you play the same person and this time come up short and lose maybe by exactly the same or a similar score. What has changed within a few days, less likely to be your technical or your physical ability but more likely your emotional state has shifted, and perhaps your opponents too. This combination could help change the result.

So – let's look at how all top athletes performing at the top of their game play to their true potential. It is known as your *Ideal Performance State* (IPS), and it is an area that many of us will have felt and experienced on a rare occasion, but often we never feel it at all.

It is often called being 'in the zone'. The more emotional control we can exert when in a stressful situation the larger chance we have of accessing this mental state. Andy Murray once stated:

"The difference between top tennis players and guys that are just below is their mental strength and belief, the ability to deal with pressure. That's what separates the best players".

Roger Federer is probably the best example, in recent years if not right now, of a player that gets into 'the zone' in many professional tennis matches. As all tennis fans will have witnessed on countless occasions how, once Federer is in 'the zone', he will hit winner after winner from anywhere on the court, seemingly effortlessly. He glides round the court like a ballerina, but strikes with the potency of a boxer.

This is the level of natural rhythm and control that players at all levels strive to achieve, but in order to do so they must take their mental tennis game to the next level.

In her memoirs, *Billie Jean,* 39-time Grand Slam champion Billie Jean King describes similar territory: "It's a perfect combination of... violent action taking place in an atmosphere of total tranquillity. When it happens I want to stop the match and grab the microphone and shout, "that's what it's all about," because it is. It's not the big prize I'm going to win at the end of the match, or anything else. It's just having done something that's totally pure and having experienced the perfect emotion, and I'm always sad that I can't communicate that feeling right at the moment it's happening. I can only hope people realize what's going on.

Two-time major-winning and Ryder Cup legend Tony Jacklin would also occasionally find himself in what he described as a 'cocoon' out on the golf course: "When I'm in this state, this cocoon of concentration, I'm living fully in the present, not moving out of it. I'm aware of every inch of my swing. I'm absolutely engaged, involved in what I'm doing at that particular moment. That's the important thing. That's the difficult state to arrive at. It comes and it goes, and the pure fact that you go out on the first tee of a tournament and say, 'I must concentrate today,' is no good. It won't work. It has to already be there."

In his autobiography, *My Life and the Beautiful Game,* soccer genius Pelé remembers a day when he experienced a calmness unlike anything he had experienced before: "It was a type of euphoria. I felt I could run all day without tiring, that I could dribble through any of their team or all of them that I could almost pass through them physically. I felt I could not be hurt. It was a very strange feeling and one I had not felt before. Perhaps it was merely confidence, but I have felt confident many times without that feeling of invincibility."

Dr Jim Loehr, the world renowned sports psychologist who worked with the likes of Jim Courier, Monica Seles and Arantxa Sanchez-Vicario, has written about the IPS and created a concentric model which makes a clear distinction of the different states of mind we can experience whilst striving to play our best tennis.

Before you can help a tennis player – whether that is yourself or someone else – it is vital to recognise how that player reacts emotionally when put under a stressful situation in a competitive match.

The Four Mental Stages

As previously stated, finding your IPS is all about *controlling your emotions*. And to get there, you first need to overcome the three outside layers of emotion that distract from your IPS, namely *tanking*, *anger* and *choking*.

Tanking

The 'Tanking' player quits trying, through frustration at their own performance, often missing shots on purpose, purposely hitting balls long or in the net and trying spectacular shots that never come off because they have stopped caring. By doing so they are attempting to rationalize that he or she didn't really lose, because they didn't try. They may do this to avoid giving credit to a rival they can't stand, or to save face by being seen to avoid failure. They are emotionally lost.

If tanking is an issue for you (or a player you work with), it can be addressed by changing the way you play the game. Avoid thinking of the outcome of 'the match' – it is too large a concept for your brain to handle in this state. Instead, focus on one shot at a time, one point at a time. Set very short term goals like winning the next point, then the next game, and continually reassess until you are in a more productive place to get back to competing. (However first you need to ask the question "Do I want to be out there competing at all?" Sometimes tanking comes from an underlying issue.)

<u>Anger</u>

This player is trying their best, but still losing, causing them to become emotionally unstable. They will be shouting out, displaying negative body language and will be using unconstructive self-talk, all of which will lead to a decreased chance of success unless the player takes responsibility and does something about this behaviour.

<u>Choking</u>

Getting nearer the centre of the circle, next comes choking. This is when you start to play your game with fear, when you are trying as hard as you feel you can, but nothing is working. You can experience choking when you are in both a winning and a losing condition. You become increasingly careful with your strokes and try and guide them into the court. You will often play in what is called your 'practice mind-set', reacting to the rally rather than influencing it, causing your movement to be clumsy, and you end up hoping for a good result rather than playing with confidence and dictating. If you are winning, you may start to protect your lead rather than continuing to play in the way that got you into the winning position in the first place.

One simple method of combating both anger and choking is using a technique known as the "Three A's", where you Acknowledge what is making you choke / angry, Assess how you will best deal with the issue and finally Apply what you have decided to be the best course of action, and then move on with your game in a better mental state. This will be covered in further detail later in the book.

Finding your Ideal Performance State

This is what we are all striving for – and when I say 'We', I mean everyone from you and me to Andy Murray and Serena Williams, and indeed every sportsperson, musician, politician, business person or any individual or team seeking to fulfil their potential.

When you are in your IPS, you are fully in control. You are able to hit the ball exactly where you want, how you want and when you want, and you are playing to your best. You are full of confidence and your strokes are happening naturally, without thinking. You can focus on picking the best tactics and strategies to keep your opponent down. You can probably vividly recall the one or two times this has happened to you!

Watch how a player like Serena Williams or Novak Djokovic, when they are playing to their best, utterly dictate the rhythm of a game and it is everything their opponent can do just to get the ball back over the net while they cruise around the base line picking shots.

The IPS is what every player is looking for. It often happens by chance, and does not last for very long. Understanding the four mental stages in which you may find yourself during a match, why they happen and how you can deal with them during matches will help you achieve the Ideal Performance State more easily, more often and will result in more wins. *So how do you get there?*

Well, as outlined in the examples above, the IPS is a mysterious and rare beast – one that can be elusive. Even the sporting greats couldn't always explain how they got in 'the zone'. So while finding it may be tricky, I can certainly point you in the right direction.

First, in order to achieve your IPS, you must break down your thinking patterns and what they lead to. In essence, the wrong thinking patterns lead to distractions, and usually come from thinking more about the past or future than the present – i.e. what you must do 'now'.

When you thoughts are continually in the past thinking of the last mistake or something you are unable to move on from this has a negative impact on your game, these negative thoughts can lead to one of the negative emotions leading to tanking, anger or choking.

Similarly, when you lose your emotional control and start to think about the future, this will lead to the 'what if' scenario and bring feelings of increased anxiousness and increased nervousness leading to playing under extra pressure.

In contrast, when you are playing the game fully focused and, crucially, in the present, it brings confidence and trust in your own ability and all you are thinking about is the here and now.

It's not the first time and it probably won't be the last time I allude to this moment, but, again, think back to Andy Murray's final game against Novak Djokovic in the 2013 Wimbledon Final. He had to overcome losing three match points, then fight back from break point down three more times, before finally winning the Championship. How did he do that? *Only* by playing one point at a time. He said it himself. Thinking about the bigger picture would have overwhelmed him, as it would overwhelm anyone.

However, before you can help yourself, it is critical that you have an understanding of what mental state you are in and what thought processes you are experiencing. Assuming we can get past the 'tanking' stage using the advice in that section, those that get angry tend to play their game too much in the past. Those that choke play the game in what I like to call the 'what if' scenario – they focus too much on the future.

Wheelchair tennis star Gordon Reid uses a very simple formula to help him discover his IPS. Just as Pelé, Tony Jacklin and Billie-Jean King did, Gordon can remember the time when he played to his absolute best. But rather than simply harking back to that day nostalgically, Gordon uses that performance as his template for every match he plays.

"I once recollected all the components of the best performance I had ever had. I described it all to my coach and we wrote down all the words and feelings I used to describe that match. Now I look at that piece of paper every day and think about it. I find somewhere quiet and try to recreate the feeling I had that day, remembering what it felt like."

By being aware and realising you have a choice, rather than leaving things to chance, you can play in your IPS more often, leading to a better performance, positive results and a more enjoyable experience on the tennis court. Every player has their own unique IPS.

Success, Trust and Confidence

Take a moment and ask yourself, 'When does my trust break down in a match and why does this happen?' If real progress is to be made, and a successful shift in your game is to occur, you have to be honest and acknowledge that working out when and why your trust breaks down, and addressing it, will help you significantly. We all have moments of doubt – but equally we can all overcome them. Only by having true trust and confidence in your game, whatever the level you play at, can you play in your IPS and achieve genuine success by reaching your potential.

Trust and confidence are the themes of this section. It may seem abstract – because trust and confidence are hard to measure – but remember we are still in 'the theory' section. The practical solutions are yet to come. So first, let's think about success, because your willingness to embrace the journey to success will pave the way for trust and confidence in yourself to grow.

Winning is more important to some than others. Many of us just enjoy playing. But the truth remains that we all enjoy winning, and that is our measure of success. The scoreboard matters more than anything else. We know that victory won't land in our lap – we have to reach out and grab it unless we are playing against a vastly inferior opponent. But is victory the only measure of success?

Firstly, we must accept that success is rarely an instantaneous event, except perhaps for winning the lottery. Success is generally achieved through sustained effort, and having the tenacity to take risks and progress gradually over a period of time.

It's natural to fear risk – as it is a step into the unknown. Most people prefer being in their comfort zone to putting their necks on the line where it might fail. So success has a price that can mean setbacks and sacrifices. It will involve hard work, and may mean going with what you believe in and not listening to others. Some people are not willing to pay that price for success. Let's dissect a couple of well-known sayings about success:

<u>"Success breeds success"</u>

This emphasises that if you surround yourself with successful people it gives you an immediate advantage over others. Similarly, if you have a number of people around you that have your best interests at heart, and you experience some degree of success as a result, this will only help to further your progress with increased self- confidence and determination.

It can be very easy sometimes to not quite reach the heights you set out for and lose your way. Sometimes you need support from others to help you pull you through. Take a look at the support network round professional tennis players next time you see them on TV. They fill several rows in a stadium! Again, look to Andy Murray and his travelling 'entourage' of coaches, advisors and even friends for a very obvious example. So in effect the saying 'success breeds success', is true.

<u>"If you fail to plan, then you plan to fail"</u>

What this means is that you must prepare for success – in order to reach your destination you have to go through the journey, and take the good times with the bad. But as long as you have a clear goal you can always get back on track.

This journey in tennis, once you set in motion a chain of events to improve your game, will become more important than the actual destination. You will learn about yourself, and it will help you find a more rounded tennis life where you have a better understanding of who you really are, where you have come from and where you are going.

So what do trust and confidence have to do with success?

Trust and confidence are two of the key areas that will allow you to bring out and master your 'A' Game, your IPS – not only in practice but under stressful match play situation. And, as mentioned, you will only achieve success – measured as performing in your IPS and fulfilling your potential, by playing with true trust and confidence.

Self-confidence is how strongly you believe in your genuine ability, at any given moment. Having strong self confidence levels can help you in a match by keeping calm and allowing you to let go of the last mistake. High, realistic self-confidence allows you to be mentally strong, and play with trust. Combine that confidence with trust, and you allow yourself to play freely, you have faith in your ability!

It is a common scenario that some players practice brilliantly yet seem to never show the same form on the court in tournaments. Often strokes which were incredibly smooth and powerful in practice become much weaker and lacking in rhythm when playing in a match for these players. Others only perform well against weaker opposition but crumble when they get challenged.

It is important to know first of all that this common problem has absolutely nothing to do with the 'physical' or 'technical' side of tennis. It's purely the mind's reaction to the pressure of the match, and it comes out in the strokes. By simply making some mental changes and allowing total trust in your ability, it will allow your results to change – and it will help you achieve the success you are seeking for.

Exercise: What gives you confidence and trust?

Go through the list below and ask yourself if you have each item in your own game / life. Only you can control your confidence levels during a performance or practice, and if you are struggling in any of these areas, take responsibility by dealing with those that need to be improved.

- A good warm up routine

- Confidence in your ability

- Previous achievements in your tennis performances (at any level)

- Proper levels of practice and conditioning

- High level of coaching

- A good relationship with your coach / coaches

- Set routines to allow you to play your best

- A well thought out game plan

- The ability to rationally and calmly debrief and implement appropriate changes.

Some of these items may seem very obvious and straightforward but, simply put, to perform to your best, all of them need to be functioning well. That doesn't mean you can't play at all unless you have them all – but we are talking about achieving optimum performance here, better than simply showing up and 'doing your best'. 'Doing your best' may be sufficient, but it isn't good enough if you know you can be better.

For example, your car will still run in the winter if the tyres are worn, the fluids are low and the heated rear-windscreen is broken – but it will hardly be at its best, or safest, for that matter. So maybe you should consider the above list as if it were like giving your car a winter service – an essential check-up to ensure everything is ticking over nicely, rather than needing to make a huge investment of time and money at a later stage. That way you know you can get on the road, or the court, with total trust and confidence that you will get the performance you require.

Exercise: When does your trust break down?

So you've had your 'winter service'. But what other risks must you consider? What issues run deeper than a superficial check-up can diagnose? Below is a list of scenarios tennis players find themselves in when trust in their own game breaks down. Read through all the scenarios and decide if any apply to your game. Being able to recognise and acknowledge this is a significant step to making changes that will help you in your game.

- When my body is tense, or when I am indecisive about my shot selection my mind has doubts or fears. I will then not fully commit to my shot it leads to choking.

- When I over-analyse a mistake, I try too hard to control my next shots, rather than trusting the skill I know I have. Therefore I start playing in a practice mind-set.

- I get frustrated or upset with my performance, causing emotions to get out of control, and I subsequently try to win my rallies faster and take less time between points, leading to increased stress levels and a poorer performance.

- I think too much about who is watching me play – my family, friends, coach, even passers-by – and I am distracted away from the game. I allow something unrelated to tennis to come into my thoughts and distract me, impacting my focus, emotions, and ultimately my performance.

- I put too much pressure on myself to win the game. I am trying to play perfect tennis, and therefore do not allow myself to make any mistakes.

Do any of these issues ring true in your game? If so, recognising them is your first move – it's easier said than done to acknowledge your own flaws, so well done!

This section has focused on looking at the 'theory' of a positive mind-set, and as such you have achieved what you need to at this point by identifying what is required to perform well and also the 'triggers' that cause you to perform below your best.

Addressing these issues will allow you to take another step towards fulfilling your potential, and the rest of *You Can Be Serious* is dedicated to giving you the tools and ideas to do so. For now, though, make a note or keep in mind the areas from the previous section which resonated with you, the ones you know affect your own game the most, and allow the rest of this book to introduce the solutions you need.

Section 3 – Getting Match Fit

Your training starts here. Now. It begins before you pick up a racket, lace up your shoes or even arrange a match. It begins on your couch, in bed, on holidays – wherever you are this very moment.

The world's top players spend hours on court every day honing their game. And as much as we would love to emulate that, it is an impossible dream for most of us, physically and financially. But being 'match fit' means more than lasting two hours on court without collapsing. The wonderful thing is that we don't even have to be present on court to be improving our game.

Be better than the professionals

Allow yourself to consider the fact that you are quite possibly a better tennis player than you perceive yourself to be; because, in Britain at least, we tend to undervalue and play down our own ability. Mind you, the achievements and attitudes of young British players like Kyle Edmund and Laura Robson are starting to change this mind-set in tennis circles, and indeed the sporting success enjoyed by all corners of the UK and Ireland in recent years is slowly changing our cultural identity. But on the whole we are still too modest.

So, let's give you an instant boost: You are, or at least you could be, on a par with the world's top tennis players in certain areas of your game. Or you may be even better. Believe it. Here's how:

Whether you are the world number one or lifting a racket for the first time, your tennis game is made up of four components, as I like to call them as the wheel of tennis: Tactical, Technical, Physical and Mental. Take a look at the diagram below-

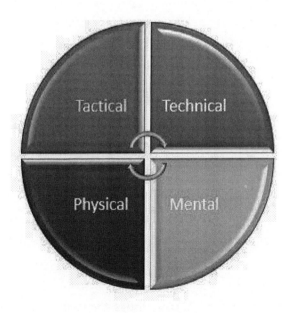

All four areas carry importance, and to play your best tennis in your Ideal Performance State you need to have all of them working together at the peak of your personal potential. Take one away and your game will suffer. Take an average club player, 'John' he is physically fit he has great tactical awareness and is mentally strong, but he has really bad technique on his serve and backhand, and tries to run round everything, is he fulfilling his potential?

A different club player 'Bill' has a good all round game with sound technique, has tactical awareness and is mentally strong, but is carrying a little too much extra weight and doesn't work on his fitness at all. If the ball comes to him he is a world beater but unfortunately if it bounces a couple of meters either side he really struggles, is he fulfilling his potential?

Another player 'Carol' is fitness mad, could run all day around the tennis court has sound technique and is mentally tough, but has no idea of basic patterns of play and has no structure in her game. Although Carol manages to find herself in winning positions she rarely converts and loses. Is she fulfilling her potential?

Finally the last club player 'Laura', she is a very fit lady, goes to lots of gym classes, has very good technique and has over the years of playing learnt the tactics of the game and which ones suit her. However when Laura is playing in a competitive match she finds herself getting nervous, holding back and choking in her game and subsequently losing to players that she feels should beat! Is Laura fulfilling her potential?

Often players will mention they have tried mental strength training in some form or another and it hasn't worked for them, maybe you are one such player. The best I can answer and to place this into some sort of context is to ask you- will you train your physicality within a gym or even better on a tennis court, and other forms of fitness but you still on occasions I am sure will pick up niggles and injuries, do you give up- no, you go away and work on your fitness to come back stronger!

Do you train your technique through lessons and practice but ultimately miss some shots and your technique lets you down in the heat of a competitive match, of course, do you give up – no. You go away and dedicate time to improving your strokes to a better skill level.

Do you practice different tactics, your patterns of play but again in a competitive match choose the wrong option and lose too many points, this happens, do you give up –no. You train more on the tactical part of the game, to ensure they stand up when under pressure.

Therefore why should your mental side of the game be any different, if a technique you are using does not have instant success, have the dedication, and strength of character to go away and practice to improve this part of your game, and ultimately enhance your tennis performance and experience? I am not stating it is vastly more important than the other 3 areas, before I annoy any physical, tactical or technical trainers, however I do say it is an important cog in the wheel to help to allow the individual to fulfil their true potential and play in their IPS more often, and is the one areas sometimes not given due diligence too!

Below is a brief explanation of what each segment means, but you might find that one of them will surprise you...

Tactical

Each player uses specific tactics within their own game style. Tactics are simply the decisions that a player makes during every rally: how, when and where to hit the ball. These decisions, when repeated often enough, culminate in a clear and successful pattern of play. These patterns can be altered between points and matches without the player changing their tactics. These shot selection decisions will be based upon such factors as a player's strengths and weaknesses, his / her opponent's strengths and weaknesses, match conditions and court surface.

Every successful player uses repeatable tactics that maximise their own strengths whenever possible. The best players don't necessarily use a wide range of tactics, they simply execute a few extremely well. Having a clear tactical focus helps any player develop the confidence and competence required to achieve their goals in tennis.

Technical

Each player must learn what is called 'shot production' – the specialised term for hitting the ball correctly – to give them the best chance of success. There is an armoury of strokes that you need to learn to allow you to play the game proficiently and cover any eventuality on court – serves, forehands, backhands, lobs, drops etc.

This is very much the area you concentrate on in the practice mind-set, when learning the biomechanics of stroke production. Aspects such as early preparation, a stable base, correct contact point and follow through all lie within the technical part of the game.

The ideal pathway for all players is to develop technically from the cognitive stage of learning (beginners, improvers), through the intermediate to the autonomous level where shots are played competently and effectively without having to think about it. But for most of us a realistic scenario is that we can execute the shot we want to play with decent consistency and reliability. Having trust in your technical ability and knowing you can play with solid and reliable stroke production allows you to focus on tactics and successfully carry out your patterns of play.

<u>Physical</u>

Tennis is a very physical sport. It is important to keep your body fit to produce your best tennis, and also to avoid any injuries. Most players play for enjoyment, but if this is causing injuries such as tennis elbow or calf strains, it can have a detrimental effect to how you can carry out others roles in your life.

Top tennis players are extremely fit, and tennis is unusual in the fact that it does not have a time limit like a lot of other sports, such as football (90 minutes) or rugby (80 minutes), so stamina is a key requirement.

The mind and body work together and the more fatigued you feel over the match, the more likely your concentration and focus will become tired, making you choose the wrong options. Therefore you need to have a combination of strength and stamina, and the optimum condition is to be as physically fresh in in the third set of a tight match as you were when you stepped on court.

<u>Mental</u>

The psychological area of the game of tennis is crucial, and the fact that you are reading this book shows that you believe it is an integral part of the game. However, actually, your mental strength is more than an 'important' aspect of your game – it is also a unique one. It is the only area where any player can hope to emulate, or even better, the world's top professionals.

All too often I have in my 20 years being involved in teaching Tennis, observed players attending lessons, you may well have had this experience. The chances are you will discuss what you want to do for the session with the coach, I will imagine in most cases that the majority of such lessons are taken up helping with problems and challenges the player is experiencing with their groundstrokes or serve. You will spend some time on the physical aspect of the game, covering movement patterns. Maybe some time on tactical patterns of play. The mental process necessary to engage the tactical, technical and physical ability – will barely get a look in.

This has to change. And it is changing, slowly, as coaches, players and parents become more and more aware of how the mental strength of a player has a massive impact on that player's success or failure in their tennis career. It is no more or less important than the others but it is an area that is just as important!

My job as a tennis coach is to help players improve – that is a broad role which goes beyond showing someone how to hit a ball. This is why when I meet a new client I ask a very straightforward question: "What can I help you with?"

It sounds very simple, but I never ask: "What stroke do you want help with?" There are four areas that make up the game and I don't want to close off three of these areas before we have even started or, worse, make the player in front of me uncomfortable, as it might be something other than the technical side of their game they want help with. It wouldn't be a particularly sound business plan in any walk of life to only target 25% of your potential customer base.

However, as I said, out of the four areas discussed the only one that a club player can hope to become as proficient as a professional is in the mental side of the game. Think for a minute and pick out your favourite player… mine was Boris Becker.

I was at an impressionable age when Becker was winning Wimbledon. I admired him and strived to replicate his playing style, his attitude and his enthusiasm for the game. But that was where our similarity ended. Looking at Boris then or now, I am nowhere close to being able to emulate his physical stature (by a good few inches), I have not had the same number of hours on court practising and playing as him, nor do I enjoy the same technical ability. But I do feel I have the same mental capacity and therefore can fulfil my own potential equally well by being mentally tough.

Think about it another way. Isn't it interesting how a number of sportsmen and women are not as perfect in real life as you perceive them to be? A lot of them, despite being peerless at their chosen sport, have failings in their personal lives that subsequently fall into the public eye – often tragically. Then, as the tales unravel to our astonishment, we realise these people are not the perfect human beings we once envisaged them as being. In many ways, and sometimes to a much more concerning degree, their mental capacity is as fragile as our own. They make errors of judgement in life on a scale that they never make in sport.

So, it is a fact that you have the same mental capacity as any professional sports person, even if you can't ever hope to rival their physical, technical or tactical prowess. If you train your mind, you can have the same, or better, mental strength as your favourite player.

But, like anything, it takes time and patience. Again, thinking back to Andy Murray's progression, it is clear to see that mental strength *can* be developed, but it *does* take time.

We all possess mental fortitude. When you first started playing tennis, if you had given up after realising it was not as easy as you thought you would not have made any improvement. It took a strong will and determination to stick in and keep trying – those are both good traits to have as a foundation to developing your mental strength.

And just like your serve or your drop shot, improving your mental strength requires discipline and practice. So, trust yourself, be confident, and strive to have the same mental strength as your favourite professional. Let's have a look at some of the ways they do it...

Imagery and the Power of the mind

There are three areas to the human mind: the conscious, the subconscious and unconscious. Your brain operates like an elevator, skipping from one area to the other to the next and back again depending on where it needs to be. Take a look at the diagram below – it shows that the part of the mind we utilise most – the conscious – is actually the smallest in terms of the number of memories it can store. This is similar to how we use technology today – we use a small device, like a smartphone, for every-day, short term functions. But when we need to focus on a bigger project, we will settle down with our more powerful laptop or PC.

The Human Mind

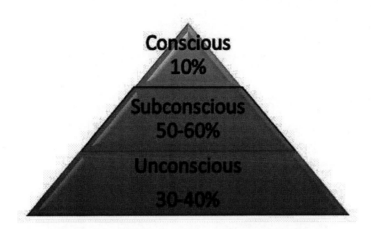

Your conscious mind uses speech, pictures, physical movement, writing and thoughts to communicate with your inner self as well as the outside world you live in.

The two main areas that distinguish and are unique to the conscious mind are the ability to direct your thoughts (e.g. Now I will think about serving a tennis ball) and the ability to imagine something which is not real (I will hit a 140mph rocket serve!).

The subconscious mind, on the other hand, plays an important role with our memory and performs the tasks we do every day without us having to actively think about it, e.g. chewing your food and swallowing it, scratching an itch or interpreting a road sign – things that happen automatically in other words –

as well as our day to day functioning (heart beating, breathing, digesting food etc).

According to the NLP communication model we are subjected to over 2 million 'bits' of data every second. Your subconscious filters out all the unnecessary information and will only allow the information that is needed at the time. It carries out this role so you can carry on performing your daily tasks without too much fuss. Imagine how difficult it would be too perform any other task if we had to remind our hearts to beat and our lungs to take in air every second of the day and night!

The subconscious can also solve problems, given time. If you ask the right question, quite often you will be provided with the solution. Sometimes you try to remember the name of a song or film and you say "it's on the tip of my tongue" but you can't quite get the words out. That's because the words you are looking for are lodged in your subconscious, while your conscious mind is prioritising the information that is more important to the time. And then, suddenly, it comes to you! This is because your subconscious has finished retrieving the answer and has transmitted it through to you.

There have been a number of times in my own experience this has worked well for me. I used to lay awake thinking about problems that I had and how to solve them, but I never really came up with anything of much use. All I would get was a shorter, more restless night. Now, I often ask myself a question, then switch off and go to sleep and let my sub-conscious work on this. In the morning, after a restful night, quite often the answer will come to me within a few hours of awakening! Our subconscious does this as logically as it is possible based on the programmes it has access to in your unconscious.

The unconscious mind is where all of our memories and past experiences are, and it is from these memories and experiences that shapes who we are, the beliefs we have and how our behaviour is formed. Our unconscious is constantly communicating with our conscious mind through our subconscious and therefore provides meaning to our life and the world around us, and communicates this through our emotions and feelings.

In a lot of ways the unconscious deals with all the same areas as the subconscious: your memory; your emotions and feelings; your behaviour. The difference, however, between the two minds is that the unconscious mind 'uploads' to the subconscious one. Think of the unconscious mind as the internet of all your memories, habits, behaviours and emotions that have been programmed and downloaded to your brain since your birth – every minutiae of detail of your life is stored in your unconscious brain, just as information is stored on the web, strewn across every inch and corner of the globe.

The subconscious, therefore, is the expert search engine that can sort through all the data, access the specific information you require and direct it towards the user – that's you and your conscious mind – enabling you to complete your chosen task. Think how amazing it is that by typing a couple of words into a search engine, you can narrow down quite literally all of the data in the world to exactly what you are looking for. Well, now you know your mind is equally as complex and efficient. So, in short, your unconscious is the World Wide Web, the subconscious is *Google*, and the conscious is you, receiving and utilising the information as needed.

Subconscious memories are closer to the surface and more easily accessible. For example if I asked you to remember your phone number, you would be able to, because it is near the surface as you use this regularly and could bring this number into your conscious thought very easily. However if I asked you to remember your first ever house phone number when you were a child you may not have the same immediate response and may struggle to remember it, as this number will still be there but a lot further down from the surface.

Now an important point is that your conscious mind is in charge of your subconscious mind – not the other way round – and will obey orders given to it by your conscious mind. The subconscious will only deliver the emotions and feelings of what you continuously think about. Again, like a search engine, it will not generate any information unless you specifically request it.

Therefore, for example, if you focus your conscious thoughts continually on negative things, then your subconscious will obediently deliver the feelings, emotions, and memories that you have associated with that type of thinking. If you are playing and feel that your serves are rubbish or your ankle is sore, then your mind will compound those feelings. Like a search engine, your mind stores up your 'search history' and become adept at predicting your thoughts.

And because those feelings will become your reality, you can then be caught up in a never ending loop of negativity, fear, and anxiety, constantly looking for the bad in every situation. Of course, with a search engine you can 'clear search history' and start afresh. It's more difficult with the human mind. This reinforces the importance of positive thinking.

I'm sure you'll agree that this is very interesting – but the other important ability of the conscious mind is the use of mental imagery. Your mind is amazing because it can imagine something new, something you've never actually experienced before.

What is Mental Imagery?

Mental imagery goes by many names and guises: visualisation, mental rehearsal and meditation to name a few. The basic techniques vary slightly but the concepts are very similar. Generally speaking, it is the process of creating a mental picture or prediction of what you want to happen or feel, and it plays an ever increasing part in sports psychology.

Or, in simpler terms, it is imagining what you will do in your head before you do it. The mind cannot tell the difference between using mental imagery and what is happening in real life. Imagery produces a response in your muscles similar to when you were doing the act in real life.

World top 10 wheelchair tennis player Gordon Reid uses imagery regularly to steady his nerves before a big play. The act of playing the perfect shot through his mind before executing it performs two functions – it helps him focus, and it also reminds him of the precise technique he needs to execute:

"I try to visualise specific shots, having the image of a perfect serve or forehand in my head. I can do it every time before I serve – it's a closed skill that I'm in control of and it helps me feel relaxed before I serve.

"But I can also use imagery to help me in open play. If I miss a forehand or backhand in a game I can go back to my imagery of the 'perfect shot' to help me refocus and get my confidence back. By doing that that I am thinking about what I need to change before playing again."

If you still need convincing, or you still don't quite understand, consider this: Jack Nicklaus, winner of 18 majors and probably the greatest golfer of all time, used mental imagery for *every* shot. In describing how he imagines his performance, he wrote:

"I never hit a shot, even in practice, without having a sharp in-focus picture of it in my head. It's like a colour movie. First, I 'see' the ball where I want it to finish, nice and white and sitting up high on the bright green grass. Then the scene quickly changes, and I 'see' the ball going there: its path, trajectory, and shape, even its behaviour on landing. Then there's a sort of fade-out, and the next scene shows me making the kind of swing that will turn the previous images into reality and only at the end of this short private Hollywood spectacular do I select a club."

An even more powerful example of mental imagery playing a crucial role in the most extreme circumstances is the tale that may have saved the life, or certainly the sanity, of Colonel George Hall. Colonel Hall was an American Prisoner of War who spent over seven years at the 'Hanoi Hilton' during the Vietnam conflict. It's a tale that's tough to forget.

During a combat mission over North Vietnam, Captain Hall's aircraft was disabled by ground fire and he was forced to eject. He was captured by the North Vietnamese and thrown into solitary confinement. In atrocious conditions, Col. Hall used the power of his mind – and in particular, imagery – to get through each day of his brutal seven-year imprisonment.

Back home Col. Hall was a keen and very able golfer, and during these long, dark, painful days in 'the hole', he would picture himself playing 18 holes on his favourite golf course. He would imagine wearing his golf gear, the feel of the club shaft in his hand, the smell of the grass, the sound of the ball pinging into the air as he struck it. He even imagined the outline of the clouds in the sky. Every detail was important for accuracy – to truly take himself to the place he dearly wanted to be. He performed this ritual every day of his capture.

Now – the punch-line hasn't come yet. Imagery did indeed keep Col. Hall stable during his years of anguish and torment as a POW. But when he was eventually released, and he returned home a hero, the true power of imagery presented itself.

Several weeks after his return, Col. Hall was still scrawny and weak from years of starvation. He needed two canes just to walk around. But when received a call from a friend inviting him to a Pro-Am Golf Tournament at his favourite golf course, he jumped at the chance. Now, this was an invite to watch the golf, not to play, but Col. Hall showed up with his clubs and insisted on playing.

Col. Hall slowly but steadily made his way round the entire course with his canes. Incredibly, he shot a 3 over par. When asked how he could possibly have done so well despite his weakened state, Col. Hall responded, "So well? I've played that course over 3,000 times in my head – 3 over par was one of my worse scores."

This may be an extreme example, but it shows the power of the mind. Col. Hall may have had more motivation than anyone can imagine to vividly picture a round of golf – but if he can do this under such harsh conditions, and then perform so well after such an ordeal, is it not a relative doddle to consider improving your tennis performance and state of mind and give it a go yourself, in a safe environment?

By continually being in charge of your own thoughts through mental imagery, and directing your focus, you can substantially influence what programme your subconscious mind constantly runs. If you persevere and work at this with enough emotional energy you can start to re-programme your unconscious and your core belief system.

The Science of Imagery

Imagery can maximize the efficiency and effectiveness of your training when used in the correct way. Top level athletes are constantly seeking for ways to gain even the smallest margin of advantage over their opponent – and they will therefore utilise every possible training technique at hand, including mental imagery, as a means to finding that extra 1% – that winning edge!

When you visualise yourself playing tennis you activate the same nerves used when actually playing the sport itself. Activating these nerves actually strengthens the connections and improves the skill, just like real practice.

Allan Paivio, a Canadian champion body builder and latterly an eminent psychology professor specialising on the human mind, identified how imagery influences sporting performance, and his framework has been the predominant guide for imagery research in sports psychology literature. Paivio indicates that imagery affects performance through both *cognitive* and *motivational* functions. The cognitive function includes strategy and specific skill rehearsal, whereas the *motivational* function consists of being successful, controlling emotions, and overcoming adversity. In other words, imagery allows you to 'practice' your tennis strokes, but even better, it allows you to do it perfectly every time!

Practising imagery can therefore build both physiological memory and confidence to perform certain skills under pressure and in a variety of possible situations. The most effective imagery techniques result in a vivid sports experience in which the athlete has complete control over a successful performance and a belief in their ability.

But – before you panic – previous experience of playing these 'perfect shots' is not necessary to create an image. As we outlined earlier, the great thing about the human mind is that it has the power to imagine things that have never happened. As a result, it is possible to imagine a specific, desired outcome, even if you have never previously achieved it. This of course won't guarantee it can happen, but the process of using imagery is another weapon in your arsenal to give your game an additional edge.

For example, the University of Chicago conducted a visualization study with three basketball teams. Team 1 was instructed to go to the gym every day for one hour and then spend one hour practicing their shooting for a month. Team 2 spent an hour in the gym every day, followed by a visualization period whereby they envisaged themselves successfully shooting hoops. No physical practice was allowed. Team 3 was instructed to play no basketball whatsoever, neither mentally or physically, for the month.

When the month had passed, the three groups were assessed to determine if their shooting had been affected. The team who had neither mental nor physical practice had, unsurprisingly, deteriorated. The team who engaged in just physical practice had a 24% improvement rate.

Amazingly, however, the team who had visualized themselves throwing successful free throws, without ever lifting a ball, had improved by 23% - almost the same margin as those who had been practicing for a month! Not only does this prove the power of imagery – it also offers the chance for any player who is injured / unable to play for a sustained period of time to ensure their game doesn't deteriorate – and indeed creates an opportunity to improve! So next time you're out of action for a while, don't sit in front of the TV lamenting your inability to play. Instead, switch that telly off and get practising!

But what about imagery in tennis terms – does it work there? The answer is yes, but how well it works seems to lie in how well the individual player embraces and engages in the imagery process.   In 2007 a team of researchers (Robin, Dominique, Toussaint, Blandin, Guillot, and Le-Her) examined the effects of imagery specifically in tennis, by observing the quality of service return accuracy in skilled tennis players.

The participants were all initially asked to complete a 'movement imagery questionnaire', to measure how good they were at 'imagining'.   The players were then separated into three groups based on their score: they were either ranked as a 'good imager', a 'poor imager', or in a control group.   Each player then physically performed 15 service returns toward a target during the pre-test to get a measure of their ability.

During the intervention phase, participants completed a rigorous series of imagery training sessions and physical trials. Then, forty-eight hours after the final training session, participants completed a service return post-test similar to the pre-test – 15 service returns towards a target. The results heralded two interesting insights: One, that the motor imagery training significantly improved the accuracy of the service returns in skilled players across the board. Second, following the imagery sessions, those deemed as 'good imagers' significantly improved their accuracy in direction to a less variable extent compared to those of lower imagery ability.

Using Imagery for Your Own Game

Of course, these scientific experiments are all very well, but how do we use imagery ourselves in an everyday context?

The obvious example is for a player to use imagery to practice a desired outcome for a particular shot, or even match or training session. Or it can be used simply to help create a relaxed sense of calm before a game.

You may have noted earlier in this chapter that Jack Nicklaus was keen to point out that even when practising, he uses imagery for every shot. Now, a game of tennis generally requires more strokes than a round of golf (though this is dependent on how good you are at tennis or how poor you are at golf!), so his habit is slightly adapted by some of the UK's top tennis players, including Colin Fleming (Commonwealth doubles champion) and Karen Paterson (winner of 7 ITF professional titles), who both emphasise the importance of imagery in the build-up to a match, rather than specifically when training.

"Before matches I used imagery," says Paterson, who retired from full-time tennis in 2007. "The evening before, in bed, I would think positive thoughts about how I wanted to play, how I saw myself beating or troubling my opponent – visualising my game plan. I already knew what I wanted to do and had made a game plan with my coach. So it was a case of visualising the positive aspects of my plan. Then before I went on court I took another five minutes to think about it."

Colin Fleming, one of Britain's top-ranked doubles player, uses imagery for a similar purpose. "I use it for match preparation and also as a mental tool to help towards achieving my goals," he states.

"For matches I like to picture the court I will be playing on and picture myself playing well on that court. For longer term goals I sometimes imagine myself competing at the level I want to get to."

Whatever it is, imagining a scene, complete with images of a previous best performance or a future desired outcome, the player is programming his or herself to simply reproduce that feeling. The key is imagining *in as much detail as possible* the way it feels to perform in what you know / envisage as your IPS – your Ideal Performance State.

The reason for this is because whether the motion you are performing is imagined or real, the brain uses the same processing function to execute it – the same neuro-pathway. Imagining yourself performing therefore strengthens the neuro-pathways that control the muscle groups required to complete the movement. So the more detailed the image, the more precise your shot or action will be in real life.

These scenarios can include any of the senses – sight, sound, touch, taste, smell. However, the most commonly used are visual (images and pictures), kinaesthetic (how the body feels), or auditory (the roar of the crowd or, as it is for most of us, the encouragement of a coach, team-mate, playing partner or loved one).

For optimal results it is best to use all three of these senses in as much detail as possible and if, for example, you can imagine your perfect serve, simply recall and repeat. And then repeat again. Using the mind, a player can call up these images over and over again, learning to create a mental blueprint for performance excellence that will train the brain for peak performance, improving the skill through repetition, similar to physical practice.

Closing your eyes and going through your best shots in your mind's eye is an ideal method of improving performance that any player can implement. You are probably doing it already as you read this, remembering that demon drop shot you played last week, or that powerful, spinning forehand you try so often but achieve so rarely. Well, just start by thinking back to those times you got it right!

This trains your mind to know what to do in certain situations and gives it triggers so that you know what to do automatically. To achieve your true peak performance, it is absolutely essential that your tennis mind is just as strong as your ground strokes. This can only be achieved through regular daily practice of your mental training, even for just a few minutes each day, through mental imagery.

When you do this enough times, your mind and body are very accustomed to the "script" and it's much easier for you to follow it. It's a great way to increase your chance of dropping into the zone and playing your best, most enjoyable and effortless tennis.

Under these circumstances, you aren't really nervous about winning and losing, because you are enjoying the process so much. You get back in touch with the whole reason for playing sports in the first place, to have fun.

How do I do it?

Often Players will say to me. "I can't visualise, it's too hard". My response is usually along the lines of, "What kind of car do you drive? Or, "What colour is the front door at your house"?

Usually, they can come up with the correct answer. I then ask, "Can you picture your front door or car?" And then I ask them to describe it as vividly as possible. The player can do this without any problem. So they are using mental imagery – they can visualise after all.

But of course, the more you use it and practice, the better you will become and the more proficient and efficient you will become at this skill. So, if you can picture your front door, you can picture yourself on a tennis court. The more detail your experience holds, the more powerful the results. You could of course source find someone trained or experienced in this area to facilitate your mental imagery – this is known as guided imagery. But to get started, go for it yourself.

When carrying out mental imagery, and to have the most powerful and long lasting results, it is important to be 'associated' when seeing yourself with your eyes closed. What this means is when you see yourself in your picture you want to imagine yourself in 'the first person' – you are seeing out of your own eyes, you look down and see your hand holding your racket, and your feet beneath you, ready to serve your first point of the match. Can you picture your own racket, tennis shoes and socks?

Good – if you have managed that then you are on the right track. But hold that thought for a little longer... Before we get deep into imagery, it's time to look at anchors and positive self-talk, because they all work best when practiced together.

Anchors and Positive Self-Talk

Now we are going to introduce imagery's best friend, the anchor. What our overall focus is on is getting yourself into the right emotional state for your tennis match. And one such way to achieve this is using 'self-talk' and having what are commonly known as 'anchors' to help keep you in the 'ACE' state of mind.

Self-talk is the talking you do in your own head to yourself, about yourself and the things that happen to you. Your own 'running commentary' on your life so to speak. Often this self-talk happens so automatically that you are barely aware of it. However, what you say to yourself can have a big effect on the way that you feel, and on what you can achieve.

Your self-talk can be like an internal coach, encouraging you, boosting your confidence, believing in you, and motivating you to achieve your goals – the proverbial angel on your shoulder. Or, your self-talk can be like the devil too of course, an internal bully, undermining you, criticising you and beating up on you when you're down. Most of us contend with both.

In tennis, self-talk can have extremely positive or negative results. Everybody has a conversation that goes on in their head. But remember, you are the master of your destiny. You can, and more importantly should, dictate how the conversation will go.

It's possible and very common to fill your head with negative self-talk. For example, something we've all seen before: You miss your first serve and you tell yourself, "don't double fault" or words to that effect. Then the mind will carry on in the form, "If I double fault I will lose the point, then lose the game. That will probably lead to losing the set, then the match. I am rubbish, I should give up and try something else".

Perhaps that's an extreme scenario – more likely these words will unfold over a game. But the conversation starts with "Don't double fault" and then it spirals from there.

Remember, if you are reading this book you are (probably) not getting paid to play tennis. It is recreational, therefore why would put yourself through this state of mind for something that you are doing supposedly for fun?

So you can change this issue in an instant by insisting upon only positive self-talk. Just as you seek to change the topic or the mood in a conversation with others, so you should with yourself. It is equally as easy to have self-talk as negative, so for a minute think about that voice in your head and what it says to you during a tennis match.

Your holy grail is to always stay confident and in control of your thoughts. Your confidence should be based on months and years of effort and good practice, so don't let one bad shot or game negatively affect your confidence, don't let it be fragile. It is vital to catch any doubts and reframe, by using positive self-talk.

So instead of saying "Don't double fault", tell yourself, "Make this next serve" or Look directly at the spot you want the serve to land and whisper, "that's where it's going." We will talk more about this particular quirk of language later in the book, but for now, as I've made clear, always remain positive!

What is an Anchor?

To preserve this positivity, and indeed to play to your peak performance, your mind needs to be in a state of calm. So, amid the stormy waters of a tennis match, we can use what is called an 'anchor' to help us maintain an unruffled, steadfast mental state. The term 'anchor' derives from the fact that its purpose is to help you to stay serene and stable on court, whatever the maelstrom that is emerging around you!

An anchor is generally an encouraging word to yourself, or using 'trigger' words on court to maintain / regain composure – a positive word or words that help you stay in your IPS (Ideal Performance State). Words like 'focus', 'calm' or 'strong'.

These should be words that are relevant and personal to you that can be quietly repeated to yourself to bring on a feeling of calm on the court. The above are examples and there are more below. Most people use affirmative words such as this, but some may use words that make them laugh or smile – the name of a child or a silly word. It doesn't matter what the word is as long as it has the effect of helping you to stay calm.

An anchor can help you regroup and refocus, to take control of the situation and get back to playing your best. So select your own personal trigger words that will "anchor" a desired emotional state and allow you to play stress free tennis. Have a look at the words below – you could select from them as your anchors, or pick ones of your own:

- Choose one word for when you find yourself getting distracted.

- Then choose the second word when you find yourself getting frustrated and angry.

Additionally, you can learn to create connections between trigger words and a desired state of concentration and focus, so as to 'anchor' that feeling and employ it whenever you need a boost to keep playing to your best.

Exercise: Putting Imagery and Anchors into Practice

Let's look at a practical way to bring mental imagery and anchors into your match play.

This exercise can be carried out the day before or on the day of a tournament or match. There is no time limit, though obviously the longer you stay with the imagery the better. Initially, I would recommend anywhere between five and 10 minutes, this is a manageable time. Avoid the situation where it starts to become a chore and your mind will switch off. Even three minutes is enough if you are used to doing it and can relax and bring the images up quickly and easily.

Before we start though, consider the power of effective breathing. One of the easiest ways to achieve a relaxed state of mind is to maintain a good flow of oxygen throughout your body to regulate your heartbeat. This can be achieved by working on your breathing technique.

Breathing doesn't just improve concentration and energy. Deep breathing also triggers the body's 'relaxation response'.

This can be extremely beneficial during tennis when you are feeling tense or nervous, just before a serve or return of serve.

We can see how important this can be when in a competitive situation, but if you are going to gain maximum effect from your mental imagery session, having your breathing working with you is vital. So, before you start the following exercise, or indeed any exercise, repeat this routine ten times, or for about two minutes, to regulate your breathing:

- Inhale through the nose for 5 seconds;
- Hold the breath in for 1 second;
- Exhale through the mouth for 5 seconds.

Each breath will make you more and more relaxed and allow any tension and stress to wash out of your body. Every time you exhale, you should feel your muscles relax more and more as you drift deeper and deeper into a state of complete relaxation. Once you have counted down from 10 to 1, you are ready for the next stage...

- Close your eyes when you are ready and continue your deep breathing. Begin crafting an image of yourself on court. Imagine looking down at your feet as you bounce the ball before serve. Feel the racket in your hand and the ball in the other. What colour / surface is the court? Are you indoors or outdoors? Is it warm or cold, windy or calm? Can you hear the familiar sound of tennis balls hitting rackets on an adjacent court? Remember what Jack Nicklaus said – like a Hollywood movie!

- Really focus on the vivid image you have created with your tennis racket on court. Now picture yourself tossing the ball up for serve, and playing your best. Be very specific, the more detail, the better the results. What are you wearing, what are you hearing, how do you feel? Make the picture colourful and bright. Make the sounds clear and the feelings real when playing your best. See yourself playing confidently, having fun and of course, winning.

AND_____/_____OR

- If there is a stroke that you lack confidence in, make sure to visualise yourself confidently and solidly playing that stroke? See yourself calmly hitting your best shots and being consistent. Visualise yourself dictating rallies, thinking one shot ahead of your opponent, hitting winners that are within your ability but are the best you are capable of.

(Don't end every point with a winner though, because the truth is that most points are won because the other player hits an unforced error. So see yourself being consistent and benefiting from your opponent's mistakes, but also hitting winners on occasion.)

- Now repeat the first word you have chosen as an anchor and repeat it over and over again. Feel good about yourself and confident in your ability. Start smiling and enjoy your performance. Totally associate this word with playing in your IPS.

- Now see your opponent mounting a challenge. They pick up their game and start returning your best shots, and forcing you into mistakes instead. But you remain calm and fight back. Picture yourself overcoming adversity and staying composed. You almost always have to do that in competition to win, so it's good to practice that. This time, use your second anchor word to associate how you fight through your fear or frustration and become calm, relaxed and on top again.

- Always end an imagery session with a positive vision, celebrating a win at the end of a match with a fist pump or maybe with friends or family. This form of successful conclusion will really fire up the mind.

<u>TIP</u>: If you lose the image or if your session is not going the way you want it to, open your eyes and concentrate on your breathing for a minute before trying to bring the images back up again. When you start these processes you may well find your mind drifts away. This is OK and totally natural because you are asking yourself to carry out a new act – so it will take practice. This is why I would suggest it is important not to try and stay with this mental imagery for too long until you feel comfortable.

This exercise, when practised on a consistent basis can offer a huge boost of confidence and self-belief. More importantly, it allows you to create a clear picture of how to win a match. With practice, you will be able to transfer the positivity and confidence that your mental imagery has instilled by using your anchors on court within seconds. I have found it possible to fire off anchors during a match and experience immediate beneficial effects.

Remember – although we are using imagery to gain an advantage and bring out our IPS on court in a competitive environment, it is vital that you use your anchors in practice too. We need skills to be practised so as they become habit –and therefore they can be transferred from practice to the cauldron of a competitive match play scenario with ease.

Using anchors to break bad habits

I recall once dealing with a younger player, a really pleasant boy who had the potential to do well; he had tennis ability, a good head on his shoulders and a very supportive family willing to give and take direction. He had a good technical and tactical game, but his problem was a psychological one: every time he made a mistake, acceptable or unacceptable, he would smash the racket on the floor. When confronted as why he did this, the player did not even realise he was carrying out this act. It had become a subconscious habit.

In order to break his habit, we agreed it would take time and effort. So, when practising, every time a mistake was made I would say "Stop" to distract the player away from what his subconscious would want to do. His habit was there to make him feel comfortable and in a safe place, but we needed to change these habits from destructive to constructive.

Much like the saying, "Give a man a fish and he will eat today, but give him a net and he will feed his family forever," my end goal was to put the responsibility into this young player's hands. Rather than solve his problem for him, I empowered him to deal with his issue by giving him the tools to doing it – in this case a positive anchor was perfect. So I allowed him to come up with a trigger word as an anchor. He could repeat it after every lost point to calm himself down.

I also another player with a similar problem the option of a 'physical' anchor to calm him until this bad habit was resolved. I asked the player to carry a small object in his pocket. Immediately after each point had finished, I told him to switch the item from one pocket to the other, therefore distracting him away from his bad habit!

This little anecdote offers a perfect conclusion to this section. The message I have been trying to get across is quite simple: By having the knowledge and understanding of how you can *control your emotions*, giving yourself the choice to do so, it puts your emotional state in *your hands* rather than leaving it to luck or chance!

Section 4 – Pre-Game

You now have a solid grounding on what it takes to ensure you can effectively control your emotions and play your own natural, free-flowing game to the best of your ability. If you were scaling Everest, you would now have made it through the foothills and past base camp. What is still to come is the hardest part – the vertical ascent – but of course at the end of it you will have reached your peak!

So now you have to start thinking about the match you will play, the strokes you will make, the techniques you will execute and how to maximise your physical potential. So let's begin by drawing up a blueprint for your game...

Game Plans

We see many professional players who are superstitious – Rafael Nadal arranging his water bottles, Serena Williams' shoe-lace tying – they feel they must perform them before they feel ready to play. Others eat the same meal or put on their kit in the same order prior to a match (Nadal always puts his headband on last, just before he walks on court). Many bounce the ball the same amount of times before serving and won't step on any white lines until the point begins.

To the onlooker, some of these habits may appear a little extreme – but whether they are or they aren't, they certainly help the player feel secure and confident. Some of us can't resist double checking that the door is locked or the tap is turned off before we go to bed – so what's the difference?

Looking at the wider picture, the superstitions of Nadal, Williams or any other player are just an extension of their game plan – a micro-second of a more detailed strategy to defeat their opponent across the net.

But a game plan is more than that. A game plan also allows you to draw a line between your 'tennis life' and your actual life. If your life and wellbeing are defined by your tennis game, there is a greater risk of low self-esteem or feeling down personally after you lose a match or perform poorly. It is important to pursue a goal of balance in life between tennis, work, friends, family and other hobbies, no matter how important you feel tennis is for you!

So if you have a game plan prior to your match, you depersonalise your performance. Your mind can accept the outcome. If you lose, it was the wrong game plan or you didn't carry out the game plan well enough – rather than chastising yourself for being a rubbish tennis player! We have all probably reflected after an unnecessarily arduous car journey that "we really should have followed the map". At least that way you could blame someone (or something) else for getting lost.

You will often hear professional players when being interviewed after a win or a defeat mention that the game plan either worked, didn't work as well as it could, or was the wrong one.

Rafael Nadal has often commented that he is the same person before as he is straight after winning a big match. He has not become a better person during the match. Similarly, we have seen Nadal lose to a comparatively 'lesser' player in the early rounds of Wimbledon for two years running (2012 and 2013). But, both times after defeat, Nadal is remarkably serene, despite his disappointment in losing. He accepts his defeat. Sometimes his obsessive personality actually works to his advantage, because he is depersonalising the defeat and realises that it is Rafa the tennis player, not Rafa the person, who has suffered a major setback.

After losing to Steve Darcis in 2013, Nadal reflected: "There were not a lot of good things for me. I tried my best all the time I had my chances but I did not make it.

"The only thing I can do is congratulate my opponent. It is not a tragedy, I lost, it is sport."

Now, if only some of us could be so objective about our game. But if one of the world's greatest ever players can do this, why can't we? Like Nadal, it is important you can leave the tennis game on the court. By all means reflect and analyse the game but do this in a controlled environment with a relaxed mind set. A game plan gives you the appropriate template to achieve this, and is remarkably simple to create.

There are two key areas that a game plan must incorporate:

1. Play to whatever you feel your strengths are. Know what you're good at, and use it. Look back at your player profile in the opening pages. Are you great at serve and volley? Is your serve your main weapon? Are you fast and get everything back? I have mentioned before that you know your game better than anybody else, so take a moment and come up with what you feel your main strengths are. You'd be surprised by how many players don't use them enough – focusing on more on being the type of player they *want to be* or *feel they should be* – rather than the *player they are*. British football fans will appreciate this folly – no doubt having witnessed their club or national team try and fail to play more like the 'continentals', rather than playing the game that suits their skill level and the British climate.

2. Play to your opponents weaknesses. Before the match starts, you want to know what parts of your opponent's game has the most weaknesses and could break down under pressure. From their ground strokes, to their weak return of serve, you want to find it and take advantage of it every chance that you get. Andy Murray is famously fond of boxing because of its 'man on man' nature. In boxing, if a player is cut or bruised, does his opponent courteously avoid targeting the injury? Of course not, he goes for blood! Tennis is slightly less violent of course, but the lesson remains the same – target the weakest point.

By using, and most importantly sticking to, the two powerful strategies above within your game plan, you'll be a much more structured player and will be giving yourself the best chance to play with the ACE approach and in your IPS.

Remember that just because you have this game plan, it doesn't mean every game will go 'according to plan'. Your opponent's perceived weaknesses may not be as fragile as you thought. Or you may yourself not be firing on all cylinders. Or your opponent may simply be better than you on the day. But the purpose of the game plan in this context isn't so much to guarantee a win as it is for you to give your game a structure and, as discussed, to 'depersonalise' your game and separate your 'individual self' from your 'tennis self'.

If your game plan works well, that's fantastic. But don't be scared to adapt it to suit a different opponent, surface or weather conditions. Likewise, don't be scared to change it if you didn't win. You may have a menu of game plans to choose from depending on the circumstances you find yourself in. As Albert Einstein said, "Insanity is doing the same thing over and over again and expecting different results"!

For any player – no matter what level you are playing at – all you have to do is keep the ball in the court one more time than your opponent. So a game plan is easily conceived and easily measured, as outlined by Colin Fleming, a world top 20 ranked British doubles-player:

"We have set targets as a [doubles] team and also vary our tactics depending on our opposition. Our set targets are related mainly to stats – e.g. our first serve percentage or percentage of points won on our first serve.

"Our tactical game plans are always based on our opponents' perceived strengths and weaknesses and how we can best play them."

Warm Ups

I want to address an area that is quite often ignored or not given the due diligence it deserves... your warm up. The warm up is such an important section of your overall match, but unfortunately amateur players often do not give the warm up the attention it deserves.

I might be a little biased, but normally male players are the worst offenders for having poor, or non-existent warm ups. They walk on court, have a couple of hits from the baseline, (usually hitting them out) before one will shout to the other, "Do you want to warm your serves up?" The usual reply goes along the lines of, "No let's just start".

I understand that in most clubs there is limited time available on court so a player must make the most of it. But how these players expect to play their best tennis when nothing is warmed up is beyond my comprehension. Though I admit I have to laugh to myself when, for the next five minutes, the tennis is mistake after mistake, accompanied with bad body language, shouting out and throwing of rackets! It amazes me how rational, intelligent adults who manage to keep the rest of their lives in control turn into a spoilt adolescent after five minutes of ill-prepared 'non' tennis.

So remember: warm ups are pivotal to you playing your best and it is what it is: a warm up. So don't expect every shot and stroke to be perfect as you are getting warmed up.

After a good warm up, all four key areas of tennis should have been addressed: the tactical, technical, physical and the mental side of your game.

Ideally you should start at the service line, exchanging hits with a softer shot allowing you to focus on you and you alone. However we don't live in an ideal world, and more often than not you may only have time to start at the baseline. Either way, warm yourself up physically and technically, focusing only on your shot production and how it feels, sounds and looks.

After hitting from the baseline for a few of minutes, and you are happy with the way you are striking the ball, start to allow yourself to bring in tactical awareness by looking at your opponent, and start to make a game plan (if you have played your opponent before you should have a good idea of what game plan you want to carry out).

After warming up your ground strokes and volleys, making mental notes of what your opponent's strengths and weaknesses are, move on to the serve and return of serve. I would recommend returning a few serves from your opponent to get the feel of their serve, as most players only return a serve for the first time once the match has started. Then warm up your own serve, always finishing on a good one!

Exercise – Utilising Game Plans and Warm ups

This little drill is great to help you develop a game plan with a friend or playing partner, and incorporates a valuable warm up too. It can be done during 'practice' or even as part of a semi-structured friendly match.

- Enter into match play with your partner, using your warm up routine to make a game plan against your opponent.
- If you are working with one other player alone, decide a way to play to make your strengths and weaknesses obvious and look for your player to pick up on these signals and make an appropriate game plan.
- You can condition the exercise by intentionally playing serve and volley or playing a very defensive game, to see if your opponent is fully focused and taking in all the signals that are being sent across the net. He / she can do likewise with you.
- Use the change of ends to address your game plan, and discuss with the player what their game plan is, is it working if not what are you going to do about it.

By answering these questions truthfully you can construct a

game plan to increase your chances of winning. Of course there are many other variables, too many for me to go through every scenario, but here are a few examples to show you what you should be thinking of:

- *Does your opponent prefer short or long rallies?*

If, for example, your opponent does prefer shorter rallies (often as a means to disguising a lack of fitness), push them out of their comfort zone by focusing on getting the ball back and keeping it in play, wearing them down.

- *Does your opponent like to take a long time or are they quick between points?*

If your opponent is fast between points, maybe try slowing the tempo down to interrupt your opponent's rhythm. If they are slow, keep them on their toes by restarting rapidly.

- *Does your opponent have a stronger or favourite side for hitting ground strokes?*

If your opponent has much stronger ground strokes on one side than on the other, play to the opponent's weaker side on big points.

- *What is the stature and physicality of your opponent?*

If your opponent is tall try to keep the ball low to make your opponent bend. If your opponent is uncomfortable at the net, hit short, then lob or make them volley.

- *What are the weather conditions?*

If it is very windy remember get up to the net when the wind is at your back and make your opponent pass you. If you are facing the wind, use backspin to float the ball and let the wind move it around.

You always have a choice in tennis, and by having a game plan you are more likely to make the correct one. Thinking and being aware of how to better your opponent at every juncture, and being totally present, can help you gain a mental edge. Commit to a plan and trust your execution!

Routines to keep you in control

As discussed at the beginning of this section, some players have a few quirks and superstitions which they like to perform during a game. I explained that these are simply part of a wider game plan, and this is true.

But while we may describe Rafael Nadal's famous nose wipe and hair tuck as a 'tick', he will simply say it's his routine.

Routines are actions you do time and time again, so as it becomes habit forming. Like cleaning your teeth or taking the same route to work each day.

Routines in tennis are important too. And, if you allow them to develop, routines can help you create a comfortable internal environment where you give yourself the best chance of success.

Routines surround your whole life on a daily basis. Take a minute and think about your average day and recognise all the routines you have: the time you get up, what you have for breakfast, the order you put your clothes on; your whole existence is full of routines.

Personally, I know for a fact that some days I get in the car and head for work, and although I am aware of what is happening around me, I often arrive at work and realise I have no recollection of the journey. This is because I have travelled the same route so many times, the actual 'travelling' part does not really need a lot of conscious effort. I had successfully completed all the manual and mental tasks required to navigate myself and my vehicle across a city alongside thousands of other motorists without even realising it!

20 years ago as a learner I would have been using the conscious part of my brain to drive. I would be thinking about needing to change gear, what gear to change to and how to execute it using the clutch and the gearstick. Nowadays it just happens 'naturally'. I certainly don't use my 'conscious' to change gears after 20 years of driving. Repetition of the correct action in any walk of life will move your ability to do so from the "Novice" cognitive through to the "Master" autonomous level of learning and performing.

If you think about yourself learning to drive or indeed learning any task or skill, you will recognise and recall your progress through the stages. For many of you, either in tennis or otherwise, you may also notice that you are only part-way along the journey!

And no matter what that ability is – from walking and talking to swinging a golf club or chopping an onion, you will know that the more you practice, and the more you develop a 'routine' to performing said task, and the better and more competent you will become.

So why is a routine important in a sport like tennis? Well, I discussed my habitual journey to work and how I can do it without thinking. But what happens if the road I take is closed, and there is a diversion? Or I have to take my wife's car because mine is at the garage? Suddenly it doesn't feel right. The journey is frustrating. The drive is 'clunky'. It's unnatural.

The same applies in tennis. If Nadal didn't use his routine, his serve and subsequent rally would then feel 'out of sync'. He would be uncomfortable and his mind would switch from the subconscious back to conscious, and he will begin thinking too much about his serve and not allowing nature to take its course. A normal point becomes and abnormal one.

The same applies in many sports. Have you ever watched rugby goal kickers? They nearly all have their own precise routine, and repeat it every time they kick for goal. Jonny Wilkinson holds his arms out in front, fists clenched, as if he were piloting an aircraft. England's Owen Farrell tilts his head to the side. In his run up, Scotland's Chris Paterson used to swing his arm vertically in the air as if he were a fast bowler. It keeps them in their comfort zone and allows them to consider every kick the same – whether it is a practice kick or a kick to win the World Cup final.

A lot of players, professional and amateur, therefore keep a physical routine – it could be your set up or the amount of times you bounce the ball prior to serving; or how you position your feet on the line.

"I bounce the ball 3 times before my first serve and twice before my second serve for no specific reason, it's just a ritual I have always had," says Colin Fleming, a Wimbledon and US Open doubles quarter-finalist.

His fellow British professional Karen Paterson, who has also played on the doubles courts of Wimbledon, uses a similar formula: "My serve routine was always to bounce the ball three times – on my first and second serve," she said, before continuing:

"When you are young you see top players do it and you don't know why, but as you get older you see that it helps to take your time. By the time I step up to serve I already know where I am serving to."

Unfortunately, many will neglect this mental aspect of their game. The mental side of a service point, for example, is without a doubt the most important aspect as it includes the decision making and confidence building skills critical to a consistent and successful serve or return. And indeed, a mental routine will complement your physical one. Your mental routine should therefore cover three areas. It should:

- Think positive thoughts - focus on imagining that perfect serve or game;
- Allow true belief in your ability and trust your game;
- Allow your mind and body to work together to produce your ideal shot or pattern of play.

Let's have a look at a couple of routines you can weave into your game very easily…

Serve Routine
Take a look at the 'ROUTINES' acrostic below. This is how I have taught my clients to develop a personal routine to help them take their time and be in the right frame of mind to

execute a serve to the best of their ability. Start away from the baseline and:

Relax your body: Shake down your arms and legs and be light on your feet;

Order your thoughts: Forget the last shot – good or bad – and focus on the here and now;

Understand: Confirm with yourself what you want to do – the type of serve, the target area;

Trust it's going to work: Keep positive (moving up to the baseline);

Imagine a perfect serve: See it go through the air and land perfectly in the target area;

Need to fully commit: Take up your position (bounce the ball, use your anchor);

Execute your perfect shot: Serve the ball or return the serve making true, solid contact;

Settle in: You have just hit a great serve. Now settle yourself into the rally.

So, by working your way through these stages with repetition of practice for your tennis routines, you will keep yourself in a safe and productive place on court.

If you feel confident doing this, you can even start preparing a routine for how you will react to your opponent's return of serve. If you get your first serve in, do they hit it back to you or straight down the baseline?   Do they usually return by forehand of backhand?

"If I knew the player I was up against I could also work out the likely return from the player and I could prepare myself for it" says Karen Paterson. So if I was getting my first serve in, I was also in control of the next ball. When it worked, I was getting lots of cheap points. Lots of third ball shots would be my winner."

Circle of Excellence

An additional small routine I also use for serving is called the 'Circle of Excellence'. It is very useful on a second serve as it is used to keep composure and regain control of your thought process.

- If you miss your first serve, imagine a small circle around you and take a step out of it.
- By stepping back, imagine you are leaving a negative space containing the missed serve;
- Now step back in with a positive outlook again.
- The benefit of this exercise is more than symbolic – it also slows the player down, allowing them to regroup. One of the main causes of double faults is rushing the second serve and not mentally being ready to deliver your best.

Return of Serve Routine

It is often the case that some players already have a pre-serve routine, which is great. However, when asking them about a return of serve routine they often look at me blankly or respond with "It depends what happens", which is a fair enough point.

But by having no idea what you are going to do, there is a greater risk of making an error. The returner needs to make a decision and execute it in a split-second, often resulting in the player not committing fully to the shot or making a mistake during the contact phase of the stroke.

Whereas if you have a return of serve routine, you set yourself up to being physically ready and mentally prepared. Let me expand. When the ball is served to you, it can only be returned by either a forehand or a backhand stroke. Therefore you can make a decision on how you intend to play the ball on the return, cutting your thinking process by 50%. If the server misses their first serve, you can step up and again have a pre-programmed response and play the ball into an area of the opponent's court you have already decided on. Thus making the response mainly down to how good your execution is rather than the decision.

Now I am not saying this will work every time. Sometimes you will face an ace or a very difficult serve to return, and you just have to get it back somehow. But that's OK – remember the server is supposed to have the advantage, all you are trying to do as a returner, especially on a first serve, is neutralise their shot and get a foothold into the rally.

By making the decision in advance, you can focus solely on the ball striking the racket and let the stroke happen without any conscious thinking, where you trust and your muscles will respond to all those hours of training and practice.

<u>Keep your routine in check – and watch the ball!</u>

Obstacles will always occur, of course, but the advantage of having a set-routine is that you can easily detect when you become distracted, because it knocks you out of your usual rhythm. When you do have a distraction it is vital you stop the routine and start the whole routine again. But that is a last resort tactic.

So, as well as having a well drilled routine I have found that a simple technique of saying 'ball' to yourself before the serve comes firing down from the opposite side will be enough to focus to mind onto what is important and stop any negative emotions of anger or nervousness.

This works equally well if you are getting distracted during a rally, if you repeat the phrase 'ball' every time you hit in a rally this will have a great effect of keeping you focused on the task at hand. It's actually the simplest form of an 'anchor' that is possible in tennis. All you are doing is reminding yourself to watch the ball!

Speaking of which, the number one most common problem I have come across when a player is trying to hit the ball correctly across the net – and the top reason why players are consequently lacking in confidence or trust in their ability – is that they don't actually watch the ball.

If I had a penny for every time I have spoken those three words, "watch the ball", to clients and players over my career, I could have retired a wealthy man a good few years ago. It's a common, obvious saying that you probably heard for the first time when your parents were teaching you to throw and catch – it's possibly one of your earliest memories.

Too often, though, it doesn't happen. Players want to see where the ball is going before they have made contact, or on contact. Unsurprisingly, the majority of miss-hits and mistakes are down to the head turning before or while the player strikes the ball.

As I keep saying to my clients, the tennis court never moves, and your opponent cannot hit the ball until it reaches their side. Therefore you have time to fully commit and finish the hitting phase of the shot before looking up. If you want a good example, have a look at Roger Federer when the cameras carry out a slow motion of his groundstrokes. This 'fixation' of the contact zone is the trademark of these elite players.

A good friend of mine is a golf professional. He will often comment on the same problem which applies to his sport: Everyone wants to see the ball in the air, everybody wants to see how good their shot is before they have finished the contact part of the swing. (I just need to watch my dad when we play golf for a great example of this!)

So it is crucially important that you have the trust to fully commit to the shot you intend to play. I have found from my teaching that when a player turns their head and vision too early from the contact point, not only is the ball not struck as cleanly but the swing path is interrupted and never finishes at the correct point.

Watching the ball is just one, albeit significant aspect of the game. And it is easy to forget about it when you are focusing on all of the different concepts outlined in this book. But now I have reminded you – watch the ball!

Exercise: Practising Your Routine

You can adapt your routine to what works best for you, as it is *you* who must be completely happy with it. But you <u>must</u> become comfortable with it for it to be effective. You could try copying Nadal's pre-serve routine if you wish, but would you feel comfortable tugging your shorts out from your behind every time you serve? I would assume not. Therefore the best time to start developing and utilising your routine is when in practice mode, to enable an easier transfer across to match play. The following are practices for having a pre-serve and pre-return of serve routine:

- Two players face across the net, one to practice the serve and the other to practice their return of serve.
- Both of you practice your own routine: talk quietly through each step so as the returner cannot hear you.
- After you are satisfied with the serve, switch ends with the serve-returner and go through the same scenario.
- Once satisfied, change roles to become the server again. Repeat the exercise.
- Now play a tie break and have a third party try to distract you as you prepare to serve / return serve. Recognise if and when you lose focus and need to start the routine again each time.
- Open the drill out to playing conditioned games, commencing at different starting points (e.g. break point up and down).
- (This can be easily adapted if you are working with only one player – when you come to playing a tie break you can still distract the player from the opposite end.)

The Practice Mind-set

People often say to me, "I am thinking too much when playing a point", and I would agree that this is a problem for a lot of players. However it's not always about thinking too much, but ensuring that you are thinking and concentrating on the appropriate areas.

When it comes to playing a match it is vital that your focus should be on picking target areas and on the best execution of hitting the ball into this area, rather than the chain of events that makes the bio-mechanics of the shot work. The key to overcoming any issue such as this is to learn to differentiate your mind-set between match play and practice.

The practice mind-set is used only for training. You are working to improve your game through a combination of coaching and open and closed drills. A closed drill is that which a coach would use in a practice session to isolate the mechanics of the shot production for technical or tactical reasons. By opening the drill up you give the player the chance to work on that execution, but also to think and make choices similar to actual match play.

Your success rate may drop initially whilst working on the shot, but in the long term you will have improved more, by using repetition of the same correct action to reinforce the learning into the muscle memory.

Performance or match play mind-set is when *trust* comes in. You have spent hours on the practice court and now it is time to trust the shot production to happen automatically, allowing full focus on the target areas and in your ability, allowing you to use your skills without thinking about the execution. Your skill will happen instinctively by relying on memory instead of consciously controlling your strokes.

This is when you are fully focused on where you are going to play the ball, commonly known as patterns of play. It relates again to the example used earlier, comparing the difference between a learner driver and one with 20 years' experience. They are performing the exact same functions with the exact same level of physical skill, but one does it on autopilot while the other needs to think through the steps.

Even having this understanding of the different mind-sets is enough for dramatic improvements in match play. Simply knowing to leave your practice mind-set on the practice court can improve your performance.

By understanding the difference between the two mind-sets you can start to gain a better understanding of how your emotions and thought processes will have to change or adapt to play your best in a competitive situation.

Exercise: The Excellence of Execution

An occurrence I see on a strangely regular basis when coaching is when a player's serve is hit just long or a rally ball is played out, but the receiver plays an unbelievably well controlled, almost nonchalant return shot – better than any shot they had played previously when the ball was still in play.

Because the rally is 'dead' and there is no threat of losing a point, the player has relaxed and subsequently played their best shot of the day. Why? Because in their relaxed, unpressurised state they are playing with no conscious thinking of the bio mechanics involved.

I will often capture that moment for the player, and emphasise to them that this is the level of 'calmness' he or she should strive to achieve when playing the point that is for real!

It is vital to trust in your skill, and let go of analysing strokes as you play. Allow your skills to happen automatically based on repetition from practice. If you are stuck in the practice mentality and overanalyse your strokes when you compete, you will limit your ability to perform to your best. When you over-analyse, you lose freedom and flow on the court.

One of the most important lessons therefore is to learn to play your tennis practically and efficiently. I have heard the word 'functional' used before when describing this, really meaning just get the job done! How often do you hear a commentator praising a top pro by saying, "she does the basics right"?

An amateur player trying to play 'perfectly' is something I come across all too often when coaching. At the end of a session I will play a few games with a client, and quite often if the player does not hit the ball well they will quickly become frustrated and annoyed. And this is despite the fact the ball is still in play and they still have a chance to win the point! But because they are not playing perfect strokes the player has mentally switched off, leading to a mistake with their next shot.

Your goal is not to play perfect, beautiful tennis. Your goal is to win. Play the game efficiently instead of trying to play every stroke perfectly. If you are trying to win the point and one of your strokes is not the cleanest, so what? Keep focused and keep concentrating until the point is over – only then should you analyse what you could do better.

The drill below will help you to learn to focus on execution during practice, which will eventually become muscle memory and second-nature in a match play situation.

This starts out as a closed drill, but gradually becomes an open drill – therefore moving you from practice mind-set into one that should replicate your mind-set during match play. The exercise is ideal for four players but can be adapted for two.

- All four players start on the baseline, one in each quadrant. Two balls will be in play and the challenge is to keep both rallies going simultaneously.

- Two players on the same side of the net each start with a ball. They hit the ball straight down the line to the player directly opposite them every time. The two receivers will always play the ball diagonally back cross court.

- The two balls go round in a figure of eight. The four players are now playing in a practice mind-set, concentrating on the best shot production to keep the rally going and fully concentrating on the technical aspect of their game.

- When one player makes a mistake, hitting the ball out or into the net, that player or the receiving player shouts out "live", and the drill changes to a competitive match play situation using the remaining ball. All four players now focus on the tactical aspects of their game looking at target areas, and on the how to win the point rather than shot execution.

- Once the point is finished, repeat the drill with the only change being the players on the two sides change the direction they are playing (i.e. the straight hitters now play the diagonal balls and vice-versa). To keep it fun and competitive, play first to 10 points.

- Adapted for two players: The players rally cross court, forehand versus forehand, or whatever technical or tactical emphasis you wish to work on when playing in a practice mind-set. As above, when a mistake is made (i.e. the ball is played short or into the wrong area) the player shouts 'live' and both revert to a match play style rally.

This will allow players to feel and recognise the difference between practice and match play mind-set. The final section below is the final piece of the jigsaw when transitioning between practice and match play.

Every Shot is the same

One of the most common problems I have encountered is players of all ages coming for a lesson and generally being content with what I have delivered, yet as they leave they say, "Great lesson, but I cannot transfer what we worked on in practice into the competitive environment of a match." In other words, when they are playing in a match with emotional significance, it creates a higher stress level that impacts their ability to execute what they have learned in practice.

In practice, we would have been breaking the player's shot down into a closed drill – isolating the volley or mid court ball.

In practice, we would work on the shot until it was perfect, open the drill a little and allow more movement and more decision making gradually, until we would both be happy.

However, despite this being a crucial part of the learning, in a competitive game you must practice caution and avoid the situation where you have that 'perfect' volley, the one you have practised again and again, to put away and find yourself using words or having thoughts to the effect of "this is my winning shot!" This can be very dangerous. You will ultimately start to concentrate on something else, as in your mind's eye you have already completed the shot and won the point. But in reality you haven't. The ball is coming towards you and you are not giving it your full attention. Invariably, a mistake is made.

Therefore you must believe you are never playing a winning shot, just a shot into an area that you have practiced time and again. Every shot should be treated the same – with the expectation that your opponent will return it. If the ball does not come back from that shot you can then celebrate that point, but allow your brain to celebrate in dead-time when nothing can hurt you.

This shift in your state of mind will allow you to play every ball, whether it is perceived as an 'easy' or 'hard' shot, to its fullest. But it also enables you to be ready for any and every ball that your opponent makes, and get it back across the net, no matter how unexpected it is.

In theory and in an ideal world this simple switch in mind-set would dramatically improve your match play. But unfortunately we do not live in an ideal world – as mentioned we are humans, not robots – and humans have feeling and emotions and mistakes will happen. So let's look at dealing with them next...

Section 5 – In Game

Now you're finally on the court. You have set your targets and practised your imagery. You trust in your own ability and are aware of your strengths and weaknesses. You have a game plan in place to beat your opponent, and anchors to calm you when something goes wrong.

But wait. It's been raining and the court is slippery. Have you accounted for that? And, hold on a minute... Oh no, it's 'club night' and there are dozens of people milling about, so you will most likely have an audience for your game. You were hoping to practice your routines without the eyes of others upon you. What will they think? Not only that, but they are waiting for your game to finish so they can get a turn on court, making you feel rushed.

Welcome to the most important part of *You Can Be Serious*. Because, as firmly as I believe in the power of imagery and anchors, the importance of a game plan and the steady influence of a routine, it counts for nothing if you can't go out and perform on the court. If you think about it, a complete tennis novice could achieve everything we have discussed up until now, having never picked up a racket. Now it's time to step up and prove yourself as a player, too...

Mistakes and Distractions

The amateur player's mind-set tends to be infiltrated by a number of obstacles that will affect his or her performance – mainly by allowing mistakes and distractions to have a detrimental effect. Unsurprisingly, then, this section of the book is quite lengthy.

You probably already have a good understanding of your most common mistakes. In my coaching experience, what I generally find is that players will have certain 'triggers' and when stress levels rise they will repeat a few mistakes on a regular basis.

As a coach, it is my job to help that individual cut out these errors. But it is still the individual – i.e. you – who knows and cares about their own game more than anybody else. Therefore, although I can help to identify issues and offer advice on how to address them, it is the player's responsibility to acknowledge the primary problem and take responsibility and control of their actions.

So I can't tell you that reading this chapter will ensure you eliminate mistakes, poor decision making and distractions from your game. But I hope it will show you the way to limiting them and improving how you deal with mistakes when you do make them. After all, even the greatest players the world has ever seen – Graf, Federer, Evert, Navratilova and Sampras – made mistakes, probably in most games!

But let's look at a subtle difference in how they manage their games compared to how you perhaps do it – you will note in its simplicity that cutting out errors and distractions may be easier than you think.

Making mistakes and being distracted are not only part of a tennis match but a part of our lives. They are normal and indeed a crucial aspect of any learning process – from walking and talking in our infancy to more complex endeavours. Think about Thomas Edison's famous quote, mildly paraphrased here: "I haven't failed. I've just found 10,000 ways that won't work".

And remember, what we are trying to achieve here is your 'Ideal Performance State'. That doesn't mean you will be mistake free and perfect – just that you are more likely to play to your best, more often.

You are only human, and the enjoyment of playing comes from winning *and also* from backing yourself to take calculated risks, and seeing them pay off. So making a mistake shouldn't always make you feel annoyed or frustrated – sometimes you accept it as the flip-side to your gamble.

Therefore, actually, it is your beliefs, thought processes and expectations that cause you to *feel* annoyed. You need to be aware of the events (specific mistakes) that cause or trigger your frustration, and have strategies already in place to deal with them.

Firstly, mistakes are subjective and graded in an unfair manner, based on other people's perceptions of what their repercussions are: For example, if a football referee gives a penalty, wrongly, against the home team, the partisan local fans will erupt with fury and anger – while the away crowd leap with joy. The referee may be harangued for that one unintentional error for weeks and months to come. But what about the players? They each made several mistakes that game, and every single other game. Yet they get off reasonably lightly in the media and their fans in comparison. We treat mistakes with bias based on *our perception* of their importance, rather than how easy or difficult they are to make.

In tennis terms, if you hit a double fault, this does not mean you should be upset! All you did was place two consecutive shots ever so slightly beyond or before your target area. It is your interpretation of what a double fault means that makes you upset. Just as occasionally stalling your car doesn't make you a bad driver, a couple of wayward shots does not make you a bad tennis player!

Hitting a double fault is not the trigger. It is your thinking process that causes you to feel frustrated. You have made a decision that a double fault will lead to you feeling frustrated.

Mistakes are part of a human being's existence, whether you are playing a tennis match, making a presentation at work or cooking the dinner, the fewer mistakes you make the better your performance and hence the better chance of success.

Think about what 2012 Olympic heptathlon champion and world sportswoman of the year Jessica Ennis-Hill said about this topic: "I'm proud of the way I've dealt with setbacks. It's hard when you feel down and you think, 'Why is the world doing this to me?' But you have to pick yourself up again. That's what makes you a better athlete."

If and when you do make a mistake, it is not always the mistake but how you deal and respond to it that matters. The mistake is already made so move past that, and work to ensure it doesn't happen again. Remember – in tennis mistakes happen, all the top players make them, but the better players will not let the mistake adversely affect their game and will be able to park the mistake and move on.

Andy Murray made his fair share of mistakes on his way to the Wimbledon title in 2013, not least in going two sets down against Fernando Verdasco in the quarter final. He looked a shadow of the player he really is at times. But grand slam tennis is a marathon, not a sprint, and he emerged as the superior player in the end. He got over those early errors and pushed on to win.

To be able to play in the "ACE" state (Always Controlling Emotions), it is vital to be able to move on and deal with a mistake in a constructive, proactive way. The alternative is to allow your stress levels to go up to a level that is detrimental to your IPS (Ideal Performance State). This can lead to shouting out negative thoughts, hitting or throwing your racket, or generally showing poor body language. If you do commit one of these 'sins', not only will it be bad for your game but it will have a positive effect on your opponent.

So firstly, let's accept that tennis is a game of peaks and troughs. When you are up your opponent is generally having a bad time, and the same rule applies in the other direction. This is why momentum in the game is seen as so important and significant.

So what I am suggesting is you limit 'the troughs', while accepting they will still appear from time to time. Stop the plunging spiral by taking action at the top of that downward turn, rather than letting circumstances run away from you and consigning yourself to another defeat.

Let me spend a little time explaining why mistakes could be happening in your game, and what distractions are getting in your way. Remember, mistakes are the *end-products*; distractions are the reasoning behind these.

Types of Mistakes

Sometimes, making mistakes is OK and you must learn to accept them. All top players make them. There is such a thing an 'acceptable' mistake. When coaching children I will call these 'OK mistakes'. Here are some examples:

- You select the correct shot and follow the right pattern of play, but just miss the line.
- You play a good shot but your opponent plays a better return.
- You play what is more commonly known as a forced error, when you are playing under extreme pressure and miss the target area due to quality of your opponent's shot.

You have to learn to accept these and let go. Move on to concentrating on the next point.

However, if your shot production is not very good and you are hitting the frame and not striking the ball clean, choosing the wrong shot or patterns of play, this is classed as an 'unacceptable' mistake. As long as you make these regularly you will play far from your best. By committing an unacceptable mistake, or what is often referred to as an unforced error, it is clear that your emotional state is not where it should be – you have lost your focus and you have allowed yourself to become distracted. You know yourself that you are a better player than your performance is currently demonstrating.

This is one of the key areas to making real progress in your mental strength training in becoming proficient in the ACE techniques. You have to become very aware of:

- Why a mistake is happening, and;
- Whether it is one you can accept and move on, or one that is unacceptable and you need to address.

Experience has shown that not accepting *any* mistakes will only lead to replaying the shot in your head and thinking about it after it has gone. By accepting some mistakes you can have closure of that shot and get back to being fully focused on the next point.

Now that you know the types of mistakes you make, let's look at their triggers – which usually boil down to distractions...

Types of Distractions

There are two types of distractions when playing the game and I like to categorize them as 'internal' and 'external' (dealing with children I call these 'inside' and 'outside' distractions).

Internal Distractions are:

- Being indecisive on what type of serve, return of serve or shot selection for a rally ball to play.
- Thinking too much on the technical aspects of your game.
- Thinking too much about what has just happened or what might happen in the future, and not concentrating on the present (here and now).
- Thinking about something unrelated to tennis – home, family, work.

These internal or inside distractions are ones that you have control over, it is your choice what you think about when playing tennis. You can think about one of the above or stay fully focused on your game, by using strategies explained later in the section.

Outside Distractions are:

- Any noise from outside the tennis court, like loud chatter or a mobile phone.
- You are put off by weather conditions you do not like.
- An opponent's bad line call.
- Losing concentration and noticing spectators watching from the side-line. This could include people you know like your parents, friends or coaches.

You have no control over these distractions so why worry about them? Why use emotional energy on something you have no control over? To play to your true potential you must focus only on areas you can control your game.

Keep in mind that even the best players in the world succumb to distraction – as illustrated in the summer of 2013 by two of the biggest names in tennis. At the French Open men's semi-final between Novak Djokovic and Rafael Nadal, it was the Serbian, Djokovic, who let distractions gets the better of him. After more than four hours of sublime tennis, the two most powerful men in the game were still exchanging blows in a stirring fifth set decider which was tied at 7-7.

But Djokovic was getting testy. He had missed several straightforward overhead smashes and was becoming noticeably agitated by the condition of the court – remarking to the umpire that it needed watering. At change of ends, after Nadal held serve to go 8-7 up, Djokovic began arguing with the umpire, Pascal Maria, about whether the court should be watered, rather than using his rest-time to regroup. Djokovic was shouting, "You are not making the decision! You are not even looking at the court! Check behind the baseline!"

This public remonstration carried on for well over a minute, with Djokovic becoming visibly more aggravated by the second. Nadal, on the other side, kept quiet and focused.

Two minutes later, Nadal was in the final, defeating the Serb 0-40 on his own serve, despite Djokovic not dropping a serve in the entire set prior to then. Of those four points that Djokovic lost on his own serve, three of them were unforced – unacceptable – errors. Remember – Nadal was playing on the same court and under the same conditions as Djokovic – only he didn't allow himself to lose his focus.

Another example involved Gordon Reid, a two time Paralympian in wheelchair tennis at just 21, and one of the top players in the world. But while Gordon may operate at the very highest level of the game now, he had to struggle his way up the learning curve just as everyone else did. Part of that process for Gordon was learning to never underestimate his opponent, no matter how apparent his superiority. An issue that no doubt plays its part in tennis at all levels.

"The matches I used to lose the most were the easier ones. I would get bored when I was a few games ahead and I would allow my mind to wander and my concentration would lapse. Suddenly I would lose a few games and be under pressure when I shouldn't be.

"So now in matches where I know I can win comfortably, I focus on other things to maintain my concentration. I am always thinking about how I can work in my goals and game plan during the match to give myself something to aim towards and focus on, such as trying to nail my angled shots. I set myself little challenges to make the game more exciting for myself."

So distractions affect all of us, and they cause mistakes as a result, as even the best players in the world have learned. However, now that you are becoming equipped with more and more knowledge on identifying and managing these distractions, you can begin to analyse your own game and behaviours and seek out what gets you under hot and bothered under normal or stressful circumstances. You may find your play is in control but an internal or external distraction is still enough to send your emotions into a heightened state of stress.

<u>Eliminating mistakes – the three- shot rule</u>

When an unacceptable mistake happens we have to analyse why it happens. One of my old coaches from school (from rugby) used to talk about his 'Three-shot rule', and I have used it ever since in my own coaching.

I certainly don't shout and scream like he did, but the principles are very simple and allow a player to take responsibility for their own actions. Before telling you about the three-shot rule, allow me to recall a junior tennis tournament I watched recently.

A young player, let's call her Jill, was in a tight match and was coming under pressure from her opponent. Rather than deal with the challenge herself, Jill was trying to ask her dad / coach where to serve and what to do during the game. Obviously this is not allowed and the dad / coach didn't really give any advice as plenty of eyes were on them. However the point is that Jill was lost on court. She could not or did not want to take responsibility for her actions. She lost (or never had) any trust in her own judgement, and was mentally very fragile.

Now, Jill was the higher ranked player for this match, and was considered far superior to her opponent, but this made no difference to the outcome. Jill had conceded any advantage she had because she was losing her confidence and not playing in the "ACE" state. She subsequently lost the match and came off in tears.

You cannot be too critical of this player, especially as she was so young, but what she needed was strategies in play to help her. If a player feels they are losing control but have something to grasp onto, they can turn the momentum around.

This example leads me on to the three-shot rule. As discussed, anyone can make a mistake, but what you must do is start to figure out what is going wrong. You can make the same mistake twice, but certainly not make it again for a third time.

By making the same mistake three-times in a row it shows a lack of rational thinking, a lack of taking responsibility, and a lack of respect to your coach and yourself. Try the three-shot rule when training – it will help you realise it is not always about finding the exact problem, but taking proactive action. Here's a few more ways to avoid mistakes...

1. Remaining Positive in Match play - Flushing

Thinking positive doesn't give you the right to win every shot – there is still an opponent on the other side of the net in charge of 50% of each rally. So if you do miss, make an error or lose a point, you still need to deal with it.

But rather than punish yourself by cursing in frustration and dwelling over each lost point in your mind, simply 'flush' it away for the remainder of the match instead. Literally imagine that shot flushing away down the toilet bowl, and your own lingering thoughts with it.

It is of course crucial that you debrief your performance and work on your weaknesses in training, but that is not an exercise for match-time. Your task for now is to win the next point and regain control. Therefore you must be fully focused on the point at hand, rather than the one that has already passed. It is gone, and so should your memory of it for now.

So by 'flushing' or 'trashing' your mistake – mentally allowing it to disappear round the U-bend or crumpling it up and throwing it in the bin – you are telling yourself that it doesn't matter for now, that it is more important to focus on what is to come, rather than what is passed. Just as I am about to move swiftly on to more positive exercises, you do likewise.

You can use flushing to complement the three shot rule – because the danger of the three shot rule is that you end up dwelling on a mistake. The key is to identify and accept the mistake – therefore lodging it as 'strike one' or 'strike two' – but then letting the thought flush away and focusing back on the game.

2. What NOT to do

This section is all about avoiding mistakes, or accepting and dealing with them when they are made. But to give yourself the best chance in a match situation, you want all thoughts of making a mistake to empty from your head.

So, as an experiment, I want you to really concentrate and *DON'T* think about a polar bear *NOT* wearing a red hat. Now, this polar bear you are *NOT* thinking about that is *NOT* wearing a red hat... it is *NOT* riding a bike either!!

This is a bizarre request I have made of you. But I can confidently predict that you are disobeying me right now - and an image of a polar bear wearing a red hat and riding a bike will have appeared in your head, at least until you gave yourself something else to focus on. You can't help yourself.

This is an issue that, here in Britain, we encounter all too often. Don't forget your toothbrush, we say, only to find ourselves buying a new one at the airport two hours later. I am not going to let this person beat me, we repeat, moments before smashing the ball into the net at match-point. We can tell ourselves 'not' to think about anything. But all that will do is focus your mind on the exact area you are trying to block out.

I used the Polar Bear example, but perhaps the most famous mnemonic for this strange trait is the 'Pink Elephant', developed by Scottish broadcaster Bill McFarlan and the central theme in his acclaimed book, *Drop the Pink Elephant*, a title aimed at losing negative thinking in favour of a positive mind-set.

After years presenting the news and sport on British television, McFarlan developed a range of tools to improve communication skills, the most pertinent of which encourages people to stop thinking and talking about things they aren't or weren't doing, and focus on the things they are doing and will do.

McFarlan, a keen golfer, recalls playing a game with his friend who kept repeating, "Don't' put the ball in the water," moments before he pinged the ball right into the middle of a lake. When Bill suggested to his partner that he instead said, "Put the ball on the green," before swinging, his luck changed.

It's a simple anecdote that clearly explains the key issue with the type of language we use – that using negatives like 'not' or 'don't' often achieve the exact opposite of what they intended, because the brain does not process the negative. It only conjures the image you are trying to avoid, and hence you do the opposite of what you want.

Taking into account that the mind tends to give you more of what you focus on, by conducting an internal dialogue with yourself involving comments like "don't double fault", "don't make a mistake" or "don't move your head", all that your mind recognises is "double fault", "make a mistake", "move your head", and that's exactly what subsequently happens. The brain cannot recognise a "don't". What it does recognise is "double fault". What we have to do is focus on telling the brain <u>what you want</u>, and <u>avoiding what you don't want</u>.

Back in the world of amateur tennis, a common problem I have heard for a number of years, is when a player misses a first serve. Generally, one of the first thoughts that enters their head is, "don't double fault" – that same sticky situation we discussed when thinking about anchors – or words to that effect. You will then do what is called 'future pace' and tell yourself, "If I lose this point I might be broken. If I am broken I will probably lose the set. If I lose the set, I will lose the match. Again!" It's a spiralling, self-fulfilling prophecy leading to the eventual, "I am rubbish at tennis. I should take up golf or something else!"

Remember – at the start of the book I mentioned what my goal is when working with a player. I give someone the mental toolkit to go out and *win* a match, rather than go out *not to lose*. A totally different mind-set.

3. The mind-set of doubles – Avoid "sorry"

Similar to using unnecessary negatives, one of the issues I see that does not help with mind-set and emotional control is when one doubles player, or both, continuously says "sorry" and apologises for every mistake.

Remember, when playing doubles you are working as a team, and your goal is to stay connected: use teamwork to give you both the best chance of success. You have to accept that a tennis match is like a rollercoaster, you will go through peaks and troughs and often when you are playing well your partner maybe going through a bad patch, and likewise the reverse.

It is vital that you feel comfortable with your partner and that you both accept your own and your team-mate's mistakes, realising nobody is perfect and mistakes will happen. If your partner is having a tough time, do not to give them corrections and try and coach them. Instead, try to change their mental state by distracting them (positively) or changing their mood (again, positively) which will quite often change their match play.

Saying "sorry" out loud will only result in your emotional state being in a place that will hinder your game. It often makes you frightened to go for interceptions at the net or fully commit to your shot. Often, a split second of hesitation is enough for the ball to fly past you. It is close enough for you to go for, but you end up paralysed, you freeze only to think, "that was my ball, I could have made that". This leads to the fear that you will make another mistake, and subsequently let yourself and your partner down.

If you are trying your best, avoid apologising to your partner. By all means apologise to your opponent if you make a winning shot by hitting the net chord or you accidently hit your opponent with a ball, but that should be it. I do however advocate plenty of noise and talking when playing. The more engaged you are with your partner, the more you can let mistakes go. Try saying at the start of the match to each other light heartedly "I am sorry in advance for any mistakes I may make – I know we are both trying our best".

Exercise: Identify your Mistakes and Distractions

The following exercises will help you get to the root of your mistakes – and aid you in weeding them out: Ask yourself to list what you feel are your five most recognisable mistakes and five most recognisable distractions when playing in a competitive match:

Mistakes

1.
2.
3.
4.
5.

Distractions

1.
2.
3.
4.
5.

Now compare both lists and see if you can pick out when you feel your mistake is caused by one of these distractions. This will start to give you a clearer understanding on the areas you need to work on.

For example your mistake may be continually choosing the wrong shot, and when you analyse this, the distraction that is causing this could be being distracted by people watching you play – you feel the need to play an impressive shot rather than the functional one. Or your mistake may be mishitting the ball. The usual solution to this one is watching it, because you are being distracted from watching the ball.

Exercise 2: Analyse when distractions occur

This is a physical drill to perform on court:

- Two players face each other across the net, and play an 'as real' tie break.
- The players recognise and acknowledge when they get distracted and / or make a mistake.
- Discuss what your common distractions are; they might be similar to each other or the same ones occurring on a regular basis. Acknowledge the difference between 'acceptable' or 'unacceptable' mistakes.
- If it is deemed an acceptable mistake move on and continue towards playing the next point.
- If it is deemed an unacceptable mistake, work out what distraction has affected your game – is it an 'internal' or 'external' distraction? Then move on and play the next point with the same routine.

As you have already learned, and will continue to learn when we look at the *Three A's*, below, there are a range of ways to avoid, overcome and deal with mistakes and distractions. They key is finding what technique or techniques work best for you.

Wheelchair tennis star Gordon Reid uses the following technique:

"Whether I win or lose a point, it gives me a burst of adrenalin and I need to calm down. So what I do is hit my hands on my racket. You will notice that Andy Murray does this a lot too, he hits his hand off the strings if he misses a shot to get it out of his system.

"I then go back to my game plan and focus on my opponent's weaknesses. This allows me to get my head back in the game and focus on what I need to do on the next point, rather than thinking about what just happened.

"There are a lot of momentum shifts in tennis. My coach says tennis is the only sport where just one point can create a total shift in momentum. So no matter how badly you are playing, it just takes one poor point from your opponent and it shifts the momentum, and you can control the match from then on."

The Three A's – Moving past Mistakes

As Gordon outlined, tennis is a game of momentum and when things start to go wrong, without the tools to address the problem, it is easy to lose a match you believed you should or could win. Likewise, one good point may turn the game in your favour.

You often hear players coming off the court making comments like, "not a good day today", or "couldn't concentrate, I wasn't with it today". Maybe it's you who says these things, it's normal. They (or you) are trying to rationalise and justify bad play – normally by offering excuses to hide behind. The answer, as always, is to begin taking responsibility and stopping the practice of using excuses as, well, an excuse for poor performance!

We have looked at avoiding distractions, but what happens when we become distracted, how do we claw our way back to our ideal performance state? Distractions will happen in life as on a tennis court, so when you notice your thoughts wandering (using the exercises outlined a couple of pages ago), you need to train yourself to assess and apply what is needed to quickly get back on track during your dead time.

There are lots of techniques – like the three-shot rule or 'flushing'. We will all respond to various techniques differently. However for me, *The Three A's* is the most powerful way to deal with mistakes and distractions within match play. The 'A's' stand for: <u>Acknowledge</u>, <u>Assess</u>, and <u>Apply</u>. So let's look at a scenario: You are in a match and you make a mistake...

- Ask yourself, "was this an acceptable mistake?"
- If the answer is yes, move on and get yourself ready for the next point safe in the knowledge you have accepted this mistake and put it behind you.
- If the answer was, "no, it was an unacceptable mistake," you need to use a strategy (the Three A's) to deal with this mistake as only when you take responsibility and deal with an unacceptable mistake can you keep your stress levels down to a manageable level, and keep yourself in a good emotional place.
- The Three A's are your safety net – something to grab in the heat of the battle...

Acknowledge what is going wrong. When unacceptable mistakes happen, recognise what is distracting you (internal or external distractions), and figure out why you are not playing with an "ACE" state mind-set.

Assess how to address the problem. Nobody knows your mistakes better than yourself. You will tend to carry out the same mistakes time and time again. It is important for you to give yourself the correction that feels right at the time, even if you choose the wrong correction! It will still have the desired effect of keeping you in the present, concentrating on your game!

Apply what you have decided will help your game, then start your pre practiced routine and / or anchor and concentrate on your tennis game again. For example, if you are miss-hitting lots of balls, you need to recognise this and tell yourself to concentrate on keeping your head still on the contact point. Or you may recognise that you are getting distracted by what is happening on the next court. Either way it is important to use the Three A's to get back to playing in the "ACE" mentality.

Exercise – Same again, but use the Three A's

- Two players face each other across the net, and play a tie break.
- The players recognise and acknowledge when they get distracted and /or make an unacceptable mistake, by using the Three A's.
- **Acknowledge** - what is distracting you? (internal or external distractions)
- **Assess** - decide how best to deal with this situation.
- **Apply** - act and get back to the present.
- An easy way to use this is when you find yourself being distracted, ask yourself this
  question: "Right here, right now what do I need to do to focus and play my best?"

- By starting to take responsibility you can start to take positive action for the better.

No player can keep focused 100%, of the time, so success boils down to your ability to Acknowledge, Assess and Apply – this will determine how well you play. A player's emotional control and ability to let go of mistakes is essential to achieving peak performance.

As previously mentioned, during the course of your tennis match you will go through peaks and troughs – but it is the player that can stay emotionally in control during a match and can manage their thoughts after a mistake that will have the better chance of playing to their full potential.

Every tennis player has the power to concentrate, but focus inevitably gets interrupted during play. Your goal is to immerse yourself in the important cues that help you play better as well as being in touch with your own personal distractions, so you can act on them quickly. *"Acknowledge, Assess, Apply"*, is your aim. It has to be a priority to focus your mind on execution when you become distracted. Stop distractions turning into lost points.

Switch on / Switch off (between points, games & sets)

Tennis is seen as one of the most psychological sports in the world. Matches can last hours, even days, and you can observe players' emotions swaying dramatically over the piece. Even within a few points of one game you can see one player's emotions range from unbridled elation to utter dismay.

Mental strength therefore plays a huge part in determining who wins the match. An important part of mental strength is stamina, as remaining focused on the 5th deuce at 5-5 in the third set can be very difficult after nearly three sets of hard fought tennis. Patting yourself on the back after the first game is all very well, but you must maintain that attitude through the entire game – even, indeed especially, when you are up against it.

Under such circumstances you must learn to remain confident, focused and in control of your emotions (the ACE state) between points, which at this point may be difficult. Tired of body and tired of mind, it is very easy to drift away for a point or two as you feel the strains and stresses of a long match. Staying focused takes discipline and concentration. You have the choice and ability, but you must manage it for the full game.

Therefore, for everyday players who can't dedicate their lives to tennis, it is vital when playing to control what I call "switch on and switch off" during a match. Your brain cannot keep concentrating continuously hour after hour. If you try, all that will happen is your concentration will switch off at the wrong moment, maybe during a crucial rally, and mistakes will unfold. Therefore you must allow your mind to have a break at times.

So, when do you give your mind permission to have a rest? The easy, but not always obvious answer is of course when a point is finished or you are at the change of ends. This is an easy and indeed purpose made moment to allow your mind a moment to refresh and regroup.

Under the official rules of tennis, you have 25 seconds from the previous point finishing to the new point starting. At a change of ends you have 90 seconds during a set and 120 seconds at a change of a set. It seems like a lot of time but some professionals still push these times to the limits.

Take a moment and time yourself for 25 seconds. Doesn't it seem an extremely long time? So between points, even if you could take less than half that time and only take 10 seconds between points, this would allow you to have your emotional state in the right place for the upcoming serve or return.

Now, of course these short respite periods help players to recover physically too – get their breath back, have a drink. But inside their heads will be working out how to overcome the person sat just a few feet away from them. And, quite often, they work something out.

Think about the 2012 US Open Final between Andy Murray and Novak Djokovic. We can only speculate what went on in those players' minds during that marathon 5-hour match, but we do know that the game fell into three very distinct phases.

Sets 1 and 2, Murray just edged both to blast into a 2-0 lead. There really wasn't much in those sets – Murray won 7-6, 7-5, the first set tie-break going to a tournament record 22 points.

Djokovic was therefore aware that he wasn't far from being able to take control, and he clearly made a mental transition between the second and third set to ensure he regained the upper hand before it was too late. And it certainly worked – he took the next two sets 6-2, 6-3. So in *120 seconds* Djokovic went from being a marginal second best to taking utter control of the match – never dropping serve and breaking Murray's. But then something else happened.

At the end of the fourth set, with Djokovic seemingly dominant beyond doubt, Andy Murray stepped out for a bathroom break. Speaking after the match, he recalled that moment, saying: "I looked at myself in the mirror and said 'Give everything on every point and leave the court with no regrets'."

He subsequently ripped through Djokovic to take the final set 6-2 and become the first Brit to win a Grand Slam tournament in more than 70 years.

While there must always be an eventual victor, as Murray was in this case, this kind of match highlights how strong the mental side of a professional player's game must be – demonstrated with equal aplomb in this instance by both those players.

Murray's coach, Ivan Lendl, supports this view and relates it directly to Murray's victory: "At some point, it's going to come down to who wants it more or how badly do you want it," Lendl said. "I don't want to say Novak didn't want it. But it's: 'How bad do you want it? What price are you going to pay and how can you execute under extreme pressure?' "

Now think about how long you normally leave between points or even a change of ends, and I bet if it is anything like what I have witnessed in amateur tennis matches this will be nowhere near the allocated time. More often players can't start a new point quick enough, or get another ball out of their pocket quick enough for their second serve!

Indeed, at the amateur level, this behaviour is even more curious at those 'pressure moments', because a player who has lost the previous point often ends up rushing to get back into play quicker, which actually leads to increased stress levels. And, as mentioned earlier, increased stress levels will ultimately result in a diminishing performance – 'Tanking', 'Anger', or 'Choking'. As you might have guessed, taking the opposite approach to this is much more productive. More often, if you actually allow yourself a few seconds to regroup, you can maintain your control, and perhaps even take control, empowering yourself to play with true trust and confidence.

Consider the example of Colin Fleming – GB Davis Cup player and Commonwealth Games mixed doubles champion in 2010. When I asked him about the importance of regrouping between points, he replied by saying that he and his partner will do it even if there is no obvious need:

"Certain things happen every time as a ritual, and certain things are dependent on the circumstances. But between every point when serving, my partner and I will discuss the placement of the first and second serve and also the movement of the net player.

"Between every point on return we make a point of coming together even if nothing is said, just for a 'high five' or 'nudge' as this helps to maintain the team energy at all times. On other occasions I may use the towel in hot conditions or we may discuss other tactical things."

In your own game, you may already have ideas as to what you might choose to do to use the time constructively. As Colin said, it's a mix of ritual and circumstance. However, to get you thinking, I would recommend asking yourself the following questions at the change of ends:

- What in my game is working for me at present?

- Is my game plan working at the minute?

- If not how can I change the momentum of the game?

Or to simplify, think of one area of your game so far that you are carrying out well and pledge to continue doing so; and then think one area you need to improve and commit to achieving that also. Then switch off for a few seconds too and allow your brain to take a break. Think about, something unrelated to the game: the weather, what you are having for your dinner, anything to give your mind a change of scene, in the knowledge that when you walk out for the next game you will switch on and start your routine afresh.

Exercise: Keeping Emotionally Focused

A question I have asked on many occasions in my classes and workshops is: "In one hour of an amateur singles tennis match, on average, how many minutes are you hitting the ball and playing the game?"

The answer, which surprises most people, even full time tennis coaches, is a maximum of 13 minutes, equating to 22%! The remaining 78% is called dead time, time between points and change of ends. Time when you can be thinking about the past: the last bad shot; or the future: the 'what if' scenario.

This is why tennis, along with golf, is seen as the most psychological sport out there. You have more time to think when the shot or stroke is over than you have when in the execution stage. So if you have all this time, it is not unreasonable, indeed it is necessary, to allow your mind to switch off for a few seconds at the change of ends. Just remain positive!

This exercise, by starting with 'the drill' and then developing 'the skill' will show how you can take a simple task (like hitting a ball) and make it harder, depending on what your thought process, stress levels and subsequent emotional state you are in at the time. It allows you to replicate the stresses of matchplay and learn how to manage your emotions accordingly. This is an on-court exercise for all levels of players. The ideal number of people is eight, but it can be adapted for as few as two.

Part 1: The Drill

- Start with a circle of players facing each other inwards. The group should fully focus on the tennis ball and only the tennis ball. Throw or bounce the ball to someone else in the group and fold your arms. That player now throws the ball to a different person and subsequently folds their arms so as a group you know who is left you can throw to. This continues until everybody has and thrown and caught the ball and the exercise finishes by the ball being thrown back to you.

- Now everybody can unfold their arms and repeat the process, ensuring to receive from and throw to the exact same person as last time. There are currently only two things to concentrate on: who you throw the ball to, and who you receive it from.

- As before, start one ball off in the circuit, let it go all the way round and continue indefinitely. But this time, feed a second ball into the circuit, a few seconds after the first. The standard of the group, from cognitive (beginners) through to autonomous (advanced), will determine how hard you want to make the drill and how many balls you want to feed in. The idea is to continue adding balls until some participants' stress levels and emotional states change, and mistakes to start to occur.

- For a beginners or improvers group, just adding more balls might well be enough for mistakes to start to happen (dropping the balls or throwing to the wrong person). The better the player and the more autonomous their stage of learning of throwing and catching, the more balls and distractions are needed for mistakes to happen.

- For an advanced group who manage the task with few problems, even with lots of balls, ask them to keep the same pace but now distract them by asking them to count back from 200 in multiples of 7. To make it harder again, randomly ask individuals what number they are on.

- To make this drill even harder, now ask the circle of players while keeping the drill going and counting back from 200 to now think about what they had for breakfast, or a similarly random question. (This drill will work even if you are with only one other player as you can take charge and change the speed of the ball and what the player has to focus on.)

This basic drill demonstrates how challenging it is to coordinate and carry out a simple action when your mind is being distracted away from the task at hand. As a result it also mirrors how your emotional state changes and stress levels escalate in a game, increasing the likelihood of an error! Finally, you will notice that even if you are concentrating and focusing on the task at hand and it is going well, after a period of time your mind will wander and you will stop concentrating on the primary action, leading to a mistake.

This is a very simple but clear demonstration of what can happen on the tennis court when your emotional state either changes through a heightened stress level, or you lose your focus and your mind drifts away. So how do we improve our ability to cope with this?

Part 2: The Skill

The progression for this drill is to bring in 'switch on, switch off time'. In other words, we now going to integrate 'the skill' of allowing our mind to have a break during a tennis match before refocusing on the next point; this can be brought into the drill by using the same format whether you are working with one player or several more.

- This time have the player/players focus initially for 30 seconds on the ball, carrying out the drill. Then call out "STOP" hold the ball, and relax for 10 seconds. Repeat this several times.

- Shorten the active throwing part to 10 seconds, and the rest time remains also at 10 seconds.

- Now alternate the active throwing time each time (40 seconds, 20 seconds, 60 seconds) but maintain the same 10 second rest time.

- The last progression is to stop for the 10 seconds switch off time each time somebody makes a mistake (i.e. a natural stoppage), then start again. We are now simulating game play. To make it more competitive you can give each participant three lives to avoid losing.

By introducing the 10-second 'rest' period and alternating the concentration time in between, we are replicating a series of rallies in a tennis match. A tennis player has to be willing and able to keep focus for varying time spans without switching off.

However when the ball is dropped or a 'stop' is called in the drill, this is like the end of a point, game or set, so by introducing the 10-second rests each stoppage, the player learns to relax the mind and switch off, and then switch back on when the task starts again.

In the drill we are in control of the length of time, but by making each one different it allows for the variables in an actual match – influenced by your style, your opponent's style, weather conditions and type of court surface.

And, speaking of 'styles', what kind of image do you portray on the court? Are you chilled and relaxed or tense and agitated? More importantly, can you opponent tell when you are tired, ruffled or struggling with an injury? We discussed earlier that, like boxing, tennis players need to 'go in for the kill' if they notice a chink in their opponent's armour. The secret to avoiding this happening to you, of course, is to not let your opposite number see you are toiling...

Body Language and Positive Self-Talk

Positive body language between points is crucial for two reasons:

- It keeps you in a positive emotional state
- It puts extra pressure on your opponent (hopefully changing their emotional state to one of doubt and negative self-talk).

Before reading on, take a minute to think about your body language...

Can you conjure images of any bad body language that you portray when things go wrong? Cursing to yourself, dropping your head, smashing your racket? If so, this has a detrimental effect – to any player playing in or wishing to play in their Ideal Performance State.

Body language is how you communicate with your opponent in a nonverbal way. Below is how effective communication works, and as you can see facial expressions, gesture and body posture makes up the largest section of the communication model.

Words 7%
Tone of Voice 38%
Facial expressions, gestures, body posture 55%

In more simple terms, your body language is the most obvious way to judge your mood and your character. How you stand, move and express yourself non-verbally is your biggest tell!

Positive body language

Below is a list of some methods top tennis professionals use to help keep in a positive mind-set, using body language. Have a read through them and make a conscious effort to bring some or all of them into your game – as many as you comfortable attempting. It may feel awkward at first but it will soon become habit.

- Clench your fist or give your side or leg a slap after you have won an important point. (Not gestured at your opponent, although you might feel this is desirable at times).
- Your movement between points and the changes of ends should at all times convey plenty of energy left in reserve. (But then allow yourself a moment to collect your thoughts once you get there.)
- Keep your body posture tall and positive and maintain good eye contact with your opponent, showing a true belief and confidence.
- Have a pre-programed routine (outlined in section 4) and take your time before you serve, showing maturity and a sense of being in control.

It is important that you celebrate good shots and accept bad ones, rather than what normally happens in amateur tennis – just accepting good shots and beating yourself up on bad ones! This is especially so if your mistakes are 'acceptable' mistakes.

Karen Paterson, who played professional tennis for a decade, recognised the importance of positive body language, even when she was suffering on the inside. She didn't want to give her opponent any advantage:

"Whether I was feeling good or not, playing well or not, or if I was shattered, I always avoided giving my opponent any clues. I didn't want them to see if I was tired or frustrated.

So to look confident I bluffed a little bit. Even if you are feeling a bit flat, it's good to get yourself going. I used to slap my legs a lot – you see a lot of players doing it. You may not believe in yourself at that very point, but you don't want to show that to your opponent. You want them to see that you are ready. The way you carry yourself can have a big impact on your opponent."

Now let's see if you recognise any of these examples of bad body language.

- Looking up at the sky or down at your feet in disgust or frustration when you lose a point.

- Throwing your racket.
- Dropping your racket and kicking it.
- Arguing with your umpire or opponent.
- Shouting (or swearing) negative comments.

I am certainly not suggesting you play with no emotion or passion. I like emotion, but I like it channelled. If your emotion is a release of frustration, that is OK. When watching professional tennis, a number of players have an outburst of emotion. If you can allow yourself to make sure your outburst is literally so – an act that banishes your negative emotion and allows you to get back into your ACE state – that is fine.

The worry, and I see this often, is that the outburst does not solve the problems but puts the player in an increasingly negative emotional state – because they are using the outburst to punish themselves rather than as a release of frustration. In this instance the release of emotion has done nothing to help, indeed on the contrary it has put the player in a downward spiral, and probably not long after there will be another outburst, as the player is really lost and 'crying out for help' for want of a better expression.

You know yourself well enough. In your case, can such an outburst release your dissatisfaction and help you move on? Or is this will only serve to worsen the situation in the match? What 'pattern' does your outburst usually set in motion?

Positive body language is certainly one of the easier traits that can almost immediately be woven into your game. But as you have been reading this book you have probably been saying to yourself, "there's a lot of stuff in here, where do I start?"

The answer to this question is to firstly decide which ideas appeal to you and you believe are achievable. Then begin to implement them into your game in a structured fashion, focusing on one at a time. To help you, this next and final section focuses entirely on goal setting and how to reach your targets, whatever they are.

Section 6: Go for your Goals

In the main sections of *You Can Be Serious* I have explained how important the mind is in whatever you decide to do. And if you tend to achieve more of what you focus on, you can start to understand how important the final area I am going to discuss – goal setting – can be. This will be the culmination of everything we have covered in *You Can Be Serious*, and will enable you to logically and methodically weave all of the ideas we have discussed into your own game and life.

Goal Setting – How to put these ideas in action

In layman's terms, a goal is simply *something you want to achieve*. And the more specific and realistic you can be and the higher you aim, the better the chance of success. All top tennis players, and indeed top performers in any field, have goals. It's what drives them on, gets them up early in the morning and motivates them to work hard.

We probably have all had goals in other areas of our lives – passing exams and tests, getting into a job or university, achieving a promotion or pay rise, owning a house or having a family.

Goal setting in one form or another has most likely influenced everyone's life at some stage, but have you ever set goals in your tennis? If so, have you set goals that are more long term than 'win the next match'? (Maybe when you were 12 you said, "I'm going to win Wimbledon" – though unless your name is Andy and you're from Dunblane we shall assume that never happened). Well, whether you have or haven't, now is the time to start.

Goal Setting 101

The first rules of goal setting are that you must know exactly what goal (or goals) you wish to achieve, and that it / they will challenge you sufficiently to make an effort.

Goals can vary hugely – from the very vague 'I want to be good at tennis' (compared to whom? Your Granny or Pete Sampras?), to the very precise – 'I want to gain a 60% successful first serve rate with 20% of those being aces'. Or, using the ideas in *You Can Be Serious*, it may be, 'I want to develop a serve and return of serve routine that I can rely on,' or 'I am going to eliminate unacceptable errors from my game'.

Those last two examples were very precise goals. And by being very specific in your goal and then setting out a series of steps to reach it, goals become a committed and manageable process. It's much easier to measure a specific goal than a vague one, and you have a clear focus on exactly what you want to achieve.

And, surprisingly, if you aim for a goal that is both specific and 'challenging' (within reason), you are more likely to benefit. Consider the following extract on goal setting from the renowned American business psychologists, Locke and Latham:

"Goals are immediate regulators of human action. A goal is defined simply as what the individual is consciously trying to do. Goals operate largely through internal comparison processes and require internal standards against which to evaluate ongoing performance. According to the theory, hard goals result in a higher level of performance than do easy goals, and specific hard goals result in a higher level of performance than do no goals or generalized goal of do your best."

"Easy goals can easily be achieved therefore there is no incentive to increase performance. Goals that are too difficult are perceived as unattainable." (Bennett, 2009). So test yourself, but allow yourself a measure of hope that you may one day complete that test.

SMART Goals

Moving on from those first two golden rules (specific and challenging) you may wish to expand your goal(s) further, and start to fill in the detail on your pathway to success. You may have seen this before, but using the formula 'SMART' is one recognised way to ensure any goal you set is both detailed and appropriate:

Specific: You must know exactly what you wish to achieve (e.g. 'win the club championship', or 'create a game plan for my next match').

Measurable: you should have a means of determining whether you have reached your goal or not. So, rather than saying 'win more matches' you would say 'win 8 of my next 10 matches', or 'work on my imagery for at least three minutes every day'

Achievable: an obvious one. Don't aim to win a Grand Slam unless you believe it is possible. Aim high, but within the bounds of what is realistic.

Relevant: equally obvious – if your goal is to get fitter, for example, make sure the training you do is related to tennis. Top tennis players are lean and muscular but they don't overdo the gym work – looking like a body-builder won't help them.

<u>T</u>imed: Give yourself a realistic time limit to achieve your goal – within short, medium or long term boundaries.

The fact is that goal setting works! Athletes use it all the time, setting themselves daily short-term goals (e.g. return 100 serves in training); medium-term goals (e.g. improve my speed over 10m in the off-season); and long-term goals (win a Slam)!

Earl Nightingale, one of the world's top motivational speakers, put it this way: "People with goals succeed because they know where they are going. It's as simple as that."

<u>Breaking down your Goals</u>

We live in a results-driven society, so most of us tend to focus on outcome goals (e.g. winning a tennis match) as opposed to process goals (e.g. staying focused and using good routines throughout the match).

The problem with this is that we have very little control over outcome goals. While I agree it is important to aim for a particular result, relying solely on outcome goals can leave you frustrated. You could have the game of your life, but still technically fail because someone else was even more prepared and played just a little better in a match or a tournament. There is not much we can do about how others perform – and we certainly can't control whether we get drawn against the club's best player in the first round of a championship!

So there are two types of goals that you want to set when playing tennis: outcome goals and process goals. Let me explain a little more about what each of these types of goal entail, because you will find that not only does it make sense to have both, but that they also complement each other very well.

Outcome Goals

Outcome goals are the end result, e.g. winning a match, being selected for a squad, achieving a ranking or rating. They are goals that depend on how you compare to others and are 'scoreboard' reliant in most cases.

Outcome goals are great to use as your motivation, but relying solely on them can make it difficult for you to get motivated in the short-term, especially if your outcome goal is so far in the future that it doesn't create a sense of urgency. It also means that you constantly risk disappointment and dejection because you are not in control of an outcome goal.

This is nothing to be concerned about, though. Many of the world's top athletes have outcome goals that they have never reached – but they still rank amongst the 'greats', reaching the absolute pinnacle of their sport. Such as Colin Montgomerie, who never won a major despite being one of the greatest golfers of his generation. Or Steven Gerrard, arguably the best English footballer of the last 20 years, but he has never lifted a trophy for his country or the Premier League title for his club Liverpool.

In most cases for most people, being realistic is the key. Messrs Gerrard and Montgomerie may disagree, as they may feel those titles that eluded them were within their reach, but most of us know what a pragmatic measure of success is in our own lives, within tennis or elsewhere.

This sentiment is reflected by British tennis player Karen Paterson, who despite enjoying a decade playing as a professional, was aware of her limits and set goals accordingly:

"My outcome goals were always realistic. Winning Wimbledon wasn't realistic for me. But I would look at my tournaments and set a goal based on my ranking and the quality of the people in it. So it may be to get to a final of one tournament, where for others just qualifying and winning the first round was good for me.

"So it was always about being realistic. My goals were all based on where I wanted to be and also where I wanted to 'peak' – perhaps on a surface that I knew worked well for my game."

Process Goals

Process goals, meanwhile, are the specific, steps, actions, technical skills and mental practices required to achieve a desired outcome – such as developing your drop shot or your accuracy from serve, or completing certain practice drills and warm ups before starting a match.

Process goals are crucial because they allow you focus you on what you need to accomplish to compete at your peak, making the likelihood of reaching the outcome goals that are most important to you much higher.

Fundamentally, and more importantly, process goals are within your control. You can't guarantee yourself that you will win the club championship (outcome goal) – but you can keep a mental promise that you will improve your serve returns (routines), concentrate more during a match (avoiding distractions) and improve your on-court fitness.

Bringing them together

This is where process goals and outcome goals complement each other – because, for example, by achieving the three process goals listed above, you can in turn significantly improve your chance of winning the club championship – although it still isn't guaranteed.

Both types of goal are important to success. With a clearly defined and desired outcome, you will always have motivation and a direction to steer yourself in. And with process goals we have a clear plan in place for getting what we want.

The important point is to know when to focus on the outcome, and when to focus on process. The combination of both will give you best chance of success. Generally, the time to think about outcome goals is prior to and after a performance, while the time to focus on process goals is during performance. If you think about winning during the match, your attention and concentration on the moment-by-moment play can suffer as you imagine the future or regret past mistakes, instead of being in the present.

One last point: it is important to have practice goals that support your process goals. Goals related to work ethic and attitude during practice are essential – e.g. showing up on time ready to go, entering your warm-up with enthusiasm and paying attention to the coach.

What goals should I set?

Sometimes it is difficult to think in detail about which goals we want to set. We know we would like to be 'better', but aren't sure what specific elements to address. Or you know want to try some of the ideas mentioned in this book, but don't know quite where to start.

So, we need to 'deconstruct' the make-up of a tennis player to get to the root of our strengths and weaknesses. Below is a brief reminder of the four key components of any tennis player's game (as outlined in section 3), followed by the six areas that make up each of those components:

Tactical – the decision making process that goes into every shot you play, thinking about where you place yourself on court and how, where and how hard you hit the ball. The six main elements of your tactical game are:

Serve and Volley	
Opponents at the net	
Approaching the net	
Both at the net	
Opponents approaching the net	
Player and opponents at the baseline	
Total score	

Technical – your ability to execute each shot you play accurately and correctly. Your technical game is broken down into the following six main areas:

Forehand	
Backhand	

Serve	
Volley	
Return of Serve	
Overheads	
Total Score	

Physical – your fitness and strength on the court, which will in turn dictate how well you perform tactically and technically. The six crucial areas of physical fitness in tennis are:

Flexibility	
Stamina	
Power	
Agility	
Footwork	
Speed	
Total Score	

Mental – your mind's ability to process the game unfolding and make decisions accordingly.

Positive Self-Talk	
Body Language	
Confidence	
Routines	
Game Plan	
Mental Imagery	
Total Score	

Write on or copy these charts and fill in for each of the sections where you feel each aspect of your own game is right now on a scale of 1-10, with 10 being the best possible. Go through the four components and give yourself for each of the six elements a score for your Tactical, Technical, Physical and Mental game. Also give yourself a total score of all six added together to see which of the four areas you perceive as your weakest.

This exercise should be carried out every six months to help you see if you feel there has been a shift in certain areas and what areas need to be worked on and incorporated into your goals.

<u>Where to start?</u>

To accomplish your goals, you need to know how to set them. Goal setting is a process that starts with careful consideration of *what you want*. If you want the best chance of achieving them, you need to make sure you have a clear view of what it is you actually do want. Too often, not only in tennis but in life, you spend more emotional and physical energy in deciding what you don't want instead.

By completing the above exercise you now know where your game needs addressed. And by reading this book I trust you will have some ideas as to how you can address them. So now get into the habit of stating your goals as statements of what you want, as opposed to what you don't want. (E.g. Rather than telling your friends "I'll be happy as long as I don't go out in the first round", say "I'm aiming to make the quarter-finals.")

Goal setting is much more than simply saying you want something to happen though. Unless you clearly define exactly what you want, and understand why you want it the first place, your odds of success are considerably reduced. By following and passing the following criteria you will have a better chance of success.

<u>Exercise : Set out your Goals</u>

- Before you start, take a few minutes to relax. Shut your eyes and picture what it is that would make your tennis life more rewarding. You could think of a number of different areas in your tennis that you want to improve. Don't worry about how it will happen, just imagine anything is possible (within reason) and spend a good five minutes enjoying the experience of all these wonderful thoughts and aspirations.

- Now you should be nice and relaxed and feeling good. Take a sheet of paper and write down all of your goals in no particular order. Label them as *process goals* or *outcome goals*.

- Now, on a new sheet, start writing in some sort of order which are your long term goals (1-5 years), then under that your medium goals (3-12 months), (which will help you achieve your long term ones).

- Underneath, write your short term goals (0-3 months). They will help you achieve your medium term goals.

- Make sure you create a realistic but challenging timeline, I have above made a suggestion on what I class as short, medium and long term goals, but by all means come up with your own, (it is your programme). Use the SMART formula to help you. Make one or two of your short term goals very easily achievable to start you off, to set you on the right path.

Below I have stated some examples of goals you could work towards:

- Tactical- To attack and hit aggressive topspin returns off my opponent's second serve.
- Technical- Learn the fundamentals and biomechanics of the slice backhand.
- Physical- Carry out a pre designed physical warm-up before each practice or competitive match.
- Mental- To use my pre serve or pre return of serve routine before every competitive point.

Finally, ask yourself these questions about your main outcome goals:

- Is the goal I want written down in the positive?
- Is this goal within my control?
- Am I doing this for myself or someone else?
- When will I know I have achieved my goal?
- What resources do I need?
- What will I lose or gain if I achieve it?

If you can answer these questions honestly and accurately, and the answers sit well with your values, you are ready to start working towards them.

My personal commitment

I.................................... truly want the above goals. I now make the decision to fully commit myself to achieving them.

Signed...................................... Date..............

Putting Goals into practice and dealing with the unexpected

Your goals are your dreams and aspirations, but written down. Now, anybody out there can set a goal by writing it down. That is the easy part. The hard part is carrying through with them. Success will come your way if you set the right goals *for you*, and you take responsibility to see them through. Writing down your goals allows you to set a path for your journey to reach a destination that initially seems too far away and unachievable. But that's why you have both outcome goals and process goals. Broken down into smaller chunks somehow does not seem quite so far-fetched and unachievable.

And you don't just write down what you want to achieve – you also have to 'plan your journey'. If your goal is to go on holidays to Spain, you will inherently understand that you will not just wake up on the beach! You must organise your travel, book time off work, pack your bags – and that's before you make your way to the airport!

In tennis terms, it is exactly the same. If your goal is to win the club championship (assuming that is realistic), you may have several smaller goals to achieve first (e.g. getting fit enough, working on your weaknesses, scoping out your opposition).

We must also remember as well that goals do not have to stand still. As you move through life so your outlook and priorities may change too. Your end goal might not change but how to get there might! (What happens if you get injured for example?) Take the example of Mark Beaumont, the Scot who perhaps took goal setting to an extreme when he decided to attempt the world record for solo circumnavigation of the globe by bicycle, completely unaided. The challenge required him to cover more than 18,000 miles, averaging nearly 100 miles per day, with many kilograms of kit in tow at all times.

When laid out like that, the goal seemed straightforward in its execution, if somewhat physically demanding – 100 miles a day, every day. But anyone who has even cycled 10 miles will tell you that things don't always go according to plan and routes get changed. Over the course of his journey, taking him through Europe, Asia, Australasia and North America, Mark encountered a multitude of challenges. They ranged from the obvious – fatigue, saddle sores, illness, flat tyres – to the downright dangerous – electrical storms, avoiding wild animals, being mugged and hit by cars or being unable to find food or shelter.

So Mark's goal-setting had to reflect that. While he always had the big 'outcome' goal – the record – in the back of his mind, his focus had to remain on the task at hand – the 'process'. On any given hour of any day, that 'process' may have been to make it up the next big hill, to arrive at a certain milestone or simply keep pedalling until he made up the necessary distance. And he accepted and dealt with the challenges that came as they arrived.

As he said to the media and in his book, *The Man Who Cycled the World*, afterwards, for Mark the task was very much about 'the journey' rather than the destination (process over outcome). In the end it wasn't just the physical challenge or the daily 100-mile ride – there was the emotional rollercoaster that went with it, not helped by days of isolation from any kind of meaningful human contact.

There were also the practical elements of Mark's everyday survival – fixing breakages, tending injuries, erecting tents and lighting fires on the roadside or wherever he chose to set up camp. And of course, he had to stick to, but constantly adapt, his tactical plan: a route on a map doesn't always translate into a passable pathway in real life, especially on a bicycle, not to mention the challenges of crossing borders in some of the world's less hospitable regions.

So if you take Mark's example, goal-setting in theory is a straightforward process – decide what you want to achieve, write it down and start working towards it. But in reality, you must be prepared for the 'bumps on the road' – literally or figuratively – and also accept that every aspect of your goal will have different elements: the physical execution of which is just one. So to avoid becoming overwhelmed, as Mark did, you must focus on the here and now, the immediate challenge, and allow the end-goal to take care of itself.

These principles should apply to whatever target you set for your tennis, whether it is an outcome driven goal – like winning a league or tournament – or a performance oriented one – like improving your backhand or perfecting your serve.

Goal Setting and Focus (Sticking In)

People give up on goals. It is easily done, and can happen for various reasons:
- They feel they are not achievable in their own eyes;
- They have made no real commitment or effort to achieve them;
- They give up too early (before they see their own progress).

As we have discussed, life is full of distractions, and goals are ineffective if forgotten. Writing your goals down will help you remember where you are trying to go and increase the likelihood that you will make better decisions. Parkinson's Law states that "work expands so as to fill the time available for its completion."

If you have six months to learn something, it'll take you six months to learn it. If you only have two months to learn it, you'll do what it takes to get it learned in two months.

Likewise, if you give yourself all day to practice, you'll waste much of it away being less focused on what you truly need to accomplish. Organise your day as such so that you only have one or two hours to practice, and you'll find yourself using that time more productively.

Goal-setting won't work if important people in your life aren't on the same page as you are. For instance, if you are working hard to stay focused on process goals but significant others in your life continue to emphasise outcome goals, such as winning the tournament, your goal-setting efforts will fall apart.

It is also important to feel in control of your goals. Ensuring that you accept and internalise goals is one of the most important features of goal setting. If players set their own goals, they will most likely internalise them. Sometimes when coaches or parents set goals for their children / players, they aren't taken seriously. By all means ask for help if needed but make sure it is what you really want and not just what your coach or parents want!

Goal setting not only allows you to take control of your life's direction. It also provides you a benchmark for determining whether you are actually succeeding, in life or on a tennis court. It's important for us to monitor how we are doing, and see what progress we are making towards the accomplishment of our end-goal. How much is still needed to work on, or are you almost there? It is vital to seek feedback from coaches, and parents or even colleagues, whose opinions you respect. When people don't achieve their goal, it is usually because they become bored or lose focus. Or maybe their goal is not what they wanted.

Sometimes you can have a dramatic breakthrough, but often a change happens over time and is a gradual drip, drip effect, until you look back and realise just how far you have progressed. Much as how a parent who spends every day with their child will not realise their growth until they look back at photographs from several weeks or months before.

I have come across people in the world, and I am sure you will have too, who love to be negative and try and put others down. They come from a position of limitations, so remembering there is no such thing as failure, only feedback, will help you give it a go and push you beyond your comfort zone, which is needed to really push forward and achieve your goals on a tennis court or in life. Remember, Lao-Tzu, the ancient Chinese philosopher once wrote that: "A journey of a thousand miles must begin with a single step". So take action now – take that first step.

It's Your Time to Succeed

OK, you are ready. I hope I have instilled my passion for getting the best out of your tennis and that I have delivered my promise to give you an easy to understand and practical read to take away and improve your game. In this final section I am going bring all the ideas outlined in *You Can Be Serious* together by giving you a check-list to have your game ready for whatever is thrown at you:

- Sit down and set realistic, yet challenging goals for yourself – both outcome and process goals. Make sure to set short, medium and long term goals and that they can be measured by having specific dates of completion. Always regularly evaluate your goals and be flexible in changing them. Be very specific about what you expect to accomplish, and set goals that are meaningful and relevant and that you are motivated to achieve. Identify the target skills that you need to achieve them.

- Allow time to relax and use mental imagery prior to a competition or match to help with confidence and create a clear road-map of what you want to happen.

- Decide on your "anchors" and practice them in your mental imagery session, as well as in practice sessions.

- Start your match with your warm-up making sure the tactical, technical, physical and mental aspects of your game have been addressed.

- Have a game plan before you start, or at least have one by the end of your warm-up.

- Start your game with your pre-serve or pre-return of serve routine.

- Use the 3A's, or flushing technique to deal with any mistakes made in your match.

- Use dead time at the change of ends to answer the following internal questions. By answering these questions you will have an idea of what needs to be changed if anything, and whether your game plan is working or not. Remember your game plan needs to be flexible if you want to alter your strategy:

  o What shots are working for me at present?

  o Is my game plan working at the minute?

  o If not how can I change the momentum of the game?

- Use the change of ends to allow yourself to relax and switch off, ready to refocus again as you walk out to start a new game.

- Enjoy the challenge and when you have finished your match, get on with the rest of your day. Reflect and learn, but do not obsess about your performance.

By bringing everything together, you can start to make a real difference to your game. You will learn how to cope with all the challenges that face every player from beginners to the best in the world – because we all make mistakes and have off-days. The difference is that you now know how to deal with these difficulties like the pros.

When it all boils down, *You Can Be Serious* is about helping you develop your mental strength – and learning that having mental strength is a combination of factors working together to help you keep calm and kick on – rather than losing your rag and the game with it.

Karen Paterson competed internationally for 10 years, winning two ITF singles titles and five doubles titles from 1998-2007. I asked Karen, quite simply, what mental strength means to her, and in a few short sentences she covers a large array of the topics discussed in *You Can Be Serious*…

"To me, mental strength is coping with different situations on court and knowing how to react to them, whether that's dealing with frustration, anger, nerves or setbacks, if things aren't going my way.

"I had certain techniques I used to stop me from rushing and thinking irrationally on court. So to get my head back into my game plan I reverted to my process goals, focusing on my strengths and my opponent's weaknesses.

"For example, I had a band on my wrist – something like a hair bobble – acting as an anchor. At any point in the match when I felt I wasn't in control, anything that was going to negate my game plan, I would flick the band. That would be my signal to regroup and do my 'between point routines'. I had a little area on the back of my court which was my 'safe zone'. I took a few deep breaths, reinforced my game plan and got back onto court."

The key point that Karen makes here is that to enable these techniques to work effectively, she has to slow her game down. Rather than rushing, she takes the time to continually reassess and refocus – even when playing doubles, which she did, twice, at Wimbledon. Often, getting into the habit of slowing down to allow these methods to take effect, is the hardest part. It won't happen overnight, it takes patience and practice.

"My game was very power based – I hit the ball hard and was very quick. So when I got frustrated I hit the ball harder and got quicker between points. So I had to practice slowing my game down. It was a difficult thing to learn to slow down and take my time. But when I did it made a huge difference to my game. But I wasn't comfortable to start with – I had to practice a lot.

"It's the same with the young people I coach now. They think they can do things they learn in practice straight away in a match. But really it takes time. You have to practice and practice. It's hard to recreate the same feeling as you have in a match, but by doing it on a practice court it become more comfortable.

Karen then summed up her message more succinctly than I could ever imagine. So much so, in fact, that I can going to use her words to conclude this chapter:

"If you want to improve, it's worth taking an hour a week to work on your game. To get better you need to practice – whether it's your forehand, your routines or whatever."

The value of the debrief

Debriefing should take place after every game – and I don't mean removing your shorts.

A good debrief means asking yourself questions about the game you just played and reviewing your performance. If you want fulfilment from your tennis, you first must learn to regularly measure how close you come to achieving your reasons for playing each time you step off court. So, perhaps in the shower or on the way home, ask yourself some questions after each time you play, addressing your 'top five' reasons listed above. Did I have fun? Did I move around enough for it to be beneficial to my fitness? Did I play well and / or improve my game? Did I see my friends? Did I win?

By keeping an eye on these things, it will keep your priorities pointing in the right direction. After your match, whether you have won or lost, remind yourself again of these reasons to put a little perspective in your tennis life.

For Parents and Coaches:

Before signing off I wanted to cover an area that maybe is not pertinent to everybody reading this book, however it is an area I feel passionate about as I would say a fair amount of my work now is dealing with juniors and I feel it is an area all too often overlooked, so please take this chapter if it relates to you with the positive intention it is meant, bringing and enhancing not only your child's but your own experience along the way!

Before you go any further… If you have a child who plays tennis, or if you coach children to play tennis… please remember: Tennis (or any sport) has to be fun!

As parents we all want the best for our children, whether that is for their personal, educational, vocational, professional or indeed sporting achievements. I trust you will agree that as a parent we should make sure we are supporting what our child wants to do, in whatever sport or activity they want to pursue.

If tennis is one of the sports your child chooses, that's fantastic. There are few sports out there, I believe, that help to develop the same resilience and independence as tennis. But I would always recommend your child also plays a team sport, to balance out the loneliness that an individual sport like tennis can bring.

Tennis offers a safe, structured outlet to have fun, make friends and develop healthy habits that will last a lifetime.

Beyond that, your child's every experience in tennis, positive or negative, is a learning opportunity for life: Each win is a lesson in respect and humility, every loss a chance to learn and improve.

Every early morning practice session is a chance to instil discipline and work ethic. Every new drill is an opportunity for your child's body and brain to develop and learn. How wonderful that a simple, fun sport like tennis can gift your child with the opportunity to learn all these crucial life skills.

You may also have dreams that your child will, of course, become a successful player. How we define 'successful' varies widely, but a career as a professional player is something many of us have wished for. This is quite possibly a dream your child shares with you – wishing they could be the next Andy Murray or Laura Robson. Good for them – it's important to aim high and believe in your own ability. But always remember the first and main reason that most children play sport is to have fun.

So perhaps if you are reading this book in order to help your child or children you coach, you should ask them to list their top five reasons for playing tennis. A recent survey of 11-15 year-olds conducted by Tennis Scotland suggested that girls are more likely than boys to play for social reasons – to meet and be with friends. Boys are more inclined to have a desire to improve their performance and be 'good' at the sport.

Even for the boys though, the emphasis should be on their enjoyment of tennis. And if they do invest a lot of effort into being as good as they can be, it's important to stress that, at their young age, performing and playing as well as they can, and continuously improving, is much more important than winning matches. In the early years there are factors beyond our control that impact which children are 'the best' and win most matches – it often comes down to their physical size and strength rather than pure tennis playing ability.

It's also worth noting, if you haven't done so already, that unless your child reaches a ranking within the top 200 places in the world, they are not going to make a sustainable living as a tennis player alone on the pro circuit.

Realistically, a player needs need to be close to the top 100, remembering a player needs to pay for a number of expenses like coaches, travel, accommodation and treatments – which puts quite a dent in the modest winnings available in the professional circuits which run below and parallel to the ATP and WTA. If they do not rise as high and bounce around the top 100 in the world you, as a parent, will probably have to bankroll their journey and career.

The following was taken from the International Tennis Federation and was an analysis of the top 30 junior boys and girls from year end 1993. This analysis showed how the top juniors had performed in the pros after four years (by the year end 1997).

<u>Women</u>

- 25% made it into the top 100

- 51% made it into the top 150

- 70% made it into the top 200

<u>Men</u>

- 26% made it into the top 100

- 53% made it into the top 200

- 61% made it into the top 300

Reaching the top 30 of the ITF Junior World Rankings is a good indicator of future success in the professional game, and therefore players aiming to become professional should try to first prove themselves in junior tennis. But even this does not guarantee a long and successful career in tennis. By this token, even being one of the top juniors in the world will only give you a 30% chance of making a good living and reaching the top 100.

And I emphasise the point 'making a good living', because a life in professional tennis does not guarantee a life of untold riches. Yes, the very best players in the world – the ones we all know by name – make millions and millions. But for the players outside of that elite few, the earnings on offer are more meagre.

On the normal professional circuit, only players within the world's top 100, perhaps 150, make any sort of living to be 'in profit' at the end of the year. Most of these solid professional players 'make money', but in the majority of cases it is more a matter of breaking even, after the expenses they incur for travel, accommodation, coaching and medical support. Even racket strings can cost £100s every year!

Now, realising how hard it would be to rise to the top 100, this should not take away any dreams your child might have for their tennis career. Moreover, it should give them a realistic view of what professional tennis is actually like for the majority of players.

This should hardly be a disincentive. Few people play tennis from a young age with the express purpose of making a living from it. But many will play because they want to compete and perform at a high level. This is still achievable. Top tennis players regularly play for their district, county, university and various clubs for a number of years, training hard, playing high quality tennis and pushing their ability to their limits. But the law of averages suggest that most will mainly play for recreation and enjoyment.

Now, we all know what Andy Murray has achieved – but his friend and contemporary, Keith Meisner from Elgin in the north of Scotland, is in many ways the prototype for the alternative tennis career. Growing up training and playing around the world alongside Andy and Jamie Murray and doubles star Colin Fleming, Scottish champion Keith enjoyed a highly successful junior career – making the world's top 100. He moved into the senior ranks and played for several years on the professional circuit while captaining Scotland in the 4 Nations Championship.

Meisner did not 'make it' in the same way that his good friend Andy did. But he has carved out a successful and satisfying career in sport – retiring from professional tennis and working as a highly esteemed tennis coach in Aberdeen and teaching secondary school PE. Here is Keith's story in his own words:

"I picked up my first tennis racket at the age of five, and I just loved the feeling of hitting a ball. I wanted to play at every opportunity and even made my bedroom into a mini tennis court, hitting a sponge ball off my wall for hours on end, imagining I was Andre Agassi winning the 1992 Wimbledon title. From a very young age I was obsessed with tennis. I had discovered the sport for myself, my parents had never played. I came to tennis through a local after-school club offering short tennis. When my parents discovered how much I enjoyed it, they decided to support me by joining me up to Elgin Tennis Club.

"As I improved, my tennis became an absolutely huge commitment for my parents. I wanted to be the very best in the country and my dream as a young junior player was to travel abroad to play and to, one day, play at Wimbledon. To be good enough to achieve that dream, I knew I had to practice every evening and compete in tournaments far and wide, most weekends because, being from Elgin, hardly anybody else played.

"I was the men's club champion by the age of ten, there were no indoor courts within seventy miles and nobody of a similar standard or age lived nearby for me to practice with. Every evening, I practiced with my Dad. He could only manually feed individual balls for me to hit back, and nearly every weekend we would drive to the central belt of Scotland or down into England to compete. The car had over 300,000 miles on the clock when it was sold.

"Family holidays didn't happen. Tennis took total priority. I dread to think how much money and time my parents sacrificed to allow me to pursue my dream of becoming a tennis player. When it became clear that being from so far north and trying to become a tennis player was near impossible, I left my home and family to live with Colin Fleming (a fellow top junior and now Davis Cup doubles star) and his family in Linlithgow. I did my third year of school there. I became Scottish junior champion at every age group.

"I went onto compete at international level, winning junior titles on three continents, reaching a junior ranking of 89 in the world. I just missed out on playing at Wimbledon, losing to Fabio Fogninni (current world top 20 player from Italy) in a close match in qualifying. I was devastated, coming so close and falling at the last. My lifelong dream was to play there.

"That same week I was awarded a tennis scholarship at Stirling University. I started to play some of my best tennis, winning Scottish Senior titles and winning my first ATP point to become a world ranked tennis player. I represented GB at University level on a tour of America – another one of my dreams. At University I was also picked several times to represent Scotland in the 4 Nations Championships.

"By this point I had no ambition to attempt to further enhance my world ranking. Realistically, I knew I wasn't good enough to become top 100 in the world at senior level. Maybe I lacked a little bit of self-belief as I didn't really think even the top 400 was a possibility. I really didn't want to spend years on the Futures tour struggling to break into the top 800, which is still extremely tough to do. The vast majority of the people I grew up playing with in juniors no longer compete. Only one truly "made it" – and that was Andy Murray. Jamie Baker did extremely well and maximised his potential. Jamie Murray and Colin Fleming have a great career in doubles.

"I may not have made it as a professional tennis player, but playing tennis growing up has benefited me so much in life. I now have a skill for life and a job as a tennis coach. I studied to become a PE Teacher, and undoubtedly my tennis skills helped me get on the course and to get a job. More importantly, I have made many good friends through tennis, who I am still close to. My tennis also allowed me to travel the world from a young age, leaving me with great memories and important life skills and experiences.

What Keith's story tells us is that it is vital to allow youngsters the opportunity to enjoy their experience of tennis – and to let them call the shots in terms of what they want. It is then your choice as a parent or coach as to how much you will support them. You can see the enormous effort Keith's parents made for him. But it was his choice first and foremost to pursue his own dream.

I have been a witness and spoken to a number of juniors that were pressurised by their parents and coaches to play more and more... and subsequently, the burden of competing so much led to burnout and most of them gave up the game as teenagers. I have since met and taught a number of players in their middle age that have come back to tennis after a number of years and really enjoy the game, because they are playing for themselves again, purely for exercise and enjoyment.

On several occasions in *You Can Be Serious* I have outlined experiences and opinions with regards to junior tennis players. Junior tennis matches can be stressful environments for a lot of junior tennis players and parents. It is an individual sport with no support from any team mates or coaches when they step onto court. They have to make their own decisions and change what they are doing if it is not working. Like I said before, this environment can create wonderful opportunities for your child to develop independence.

However this is itself a steep learning curve. Initially, most young players do not have the confidence to take the responsibility to make changes to their own game. Often I see an outburst of emotions on court, and after the match I will often see crying.

On occasion I will even witness parents remonstrating with their child the second he / she steps off the court! This happens in all sports. However tennis, and tennis parents, are unfortunately notorious around the world.

Tennis is and should be played by children to enhance their lives, to learn skills, for fitness, for competition, to build self-confidence and self-esteem, and to teach self-discipline, self-reliance and respect, all of which are important, but the main aim for any child has to be for fun and enjoyment.

This sometimes gets lost in the competitive structure of ratings and rankings. Whether you are a parent that knows very little or a parent that knows a lot about tennis, there's a big difference between learning the basic strokes to play the game at recreational level, and competing successfully at a high level. Problems occur with juniors because too often, the demands that competitive tennis places on them are testing their emotional control and putting them under pressure that they haven't yet learned to cope with.

I am a new parent myself, so I understand how annoying it can be when other people tell me how I should and shouldn't be raising my child. But I still always appreciate advice from people, especially if they have experience to back their opinions, so please take what I am about to say as such:

A parent knows best how to deal with their own children. You will know your child's mind-set better than anyone. As a parent you want to help your child to be happy and will encourage them in any situation they find themselves in. So I am only sharing with you some ideas that might be worth thinking about. It's hard being a good parent and even harder being a tennis parent at times, especially when you only want the best for your child.

You may often suffer from conflicting opinions – especially when thinking about how strong a role to play in influencing your children's choices, whether in school, sport or other interests. I have witnessed this conflict first hand. I have seen parents get it right, and others get it wrong. I have seen many tennis parents say things and make decisions that have not always helped the mental state of their child.

The support you show your child and how interested you are is crucial to the child's continued participation, and as a parent you have a very important role, whatever the level your child plays at in tennis.

It is about striking a balance and ensuring not to over-pressurise your child, as much of the child's emotional stress can be caused by a well-meaning but unaware parent. As discussed, this can sometimes lead to burnout, and continued pressure can even damage and put extra strain on the parent-child relationship. Below are a few observations and suggestions. I would recommend you follow these as best as you can, to allow your child to play the game with freedom and enjoyment, which will increase the chance of them playing to their best while still enjoying their tennis.

Freedom and Free Will

Your child wants love and support for what they are doing in their tennis life. Ask them if they like you watching them play, and listen to them. Take on board what their opinion is. Realise that your child not only has the right to participate in tennis but also, to choose not to participate if their desire and enjoyment has gone.

If they do want to stop, give them a break to see if they miss competing. I always say there is a time for serious coaching, training and competition, but they need to have fun and play without pressure as well.

Parents parent, coaches coach

It takes emotional control to be a good tennis parent, but it is important to make sure you stick to your parental role. Avoid being your child's coach by adhering to the following:

- Make sure you have established clear lines of communication and try to meet regularly with your child's coach to ask about your their development.

- Understand that your child's coach is a qualified professional who can help your child in many areas, both tennis and others, and also help you understand more about tennis.

- Assist the coach by helping them gain a better understanding of your child's personality and feelings. This is the one area you have a huge input into as you decide who teaches your child. Make sure you are happy with your choice.

Distractions

Again and again in this book, we will look at how distractions influence tennis performance negatively, and how cutting them out can improve your game immeasurably. Well, when speaking to junior players, especially 8-12 year olds, when I talk to them about outside distractions it comes out that their parents watching them is one of the main and most common distractions affecting the player.

A lot of the time I see lines of parents watching their child. This is natural – you want to see how well they are doing, but remember it is not all about you, it is about allowing your child to play their best. If they play better with you not directly watching, move away. Watch from a distance, or go and have a coffee and see them at the end of the match. Enjoy the break from being a mum or dad for an hour!

Body Language

If you want to watch your child's matches, and your child wants you to watch them, that's great. Watch their match... but be aware of your body language. Firstly, if your child wants you to watch their match, emphasise to them they must concentrate only on their match.

But the way in which <u>you</u> conduct yourself, verbally and non-verbally, is equally crucial. As mentioned in an earlier chapter, how one human reads another is as follows:

- 7% - your words

- 38% - your tone of voice

- 55% - your facial expression, gesture and body language

Remember you are there because you love them and want to support them, rather than to judge them. If they do look across, always give them positive body language, regardless of how they are doing: smile, nod, thumbs up – whatever you feel comfortable with but make sure you are portraying support. An encouraging look or hand clap will boost your child's morale and hearten their spirit no end.

On the other hand, dropping your head in disappointment or a negative exclamation will send your child into despair. Remember – for every single negative gesture you direct towards your child, verbal or non-verbal, it takes up to five positive ones to balance that equilibrium. That means that it takes five positive gestures just to get your child back to 'base level', and it will take more on top of that to boost their confidence. So you can see it *really* isn't worth the effort outwardly expressing your disappointment.

Unfortunately I have all too often witnessed the impact of negative body language on the side-lines. Parents conveying awful body language, shouting out, shaking their head, looking to the sky, pacing up and down, and walking away when they see a bad shot.

Bear in mind for a player to play their best, they have to be fully focussed on what is happening on the tennis court. Too often I will see the child looking towards their parent(s) after every mistake, sometimes after every point, sometimes even during a rally! And every time they look, they see their parent(s) displaying negative body language.

If they spend more time looking across to see if they have annoyed or disappointed their parent rather than concentrating on what they are doing in front of them on court, what is that doing to the child's mental state?

This is often because a parent expects their child to perform as flawlessly as the professionals. Yet, ironically, when you watch Andy Murray play or GB in the Davis Cup, often the camera will show the support team sitting in the stand watching. Whether it is after a great shot or after a mistake you will always see the same thing from a player's or team's crew: positive body language, helping and encouraging the player.

The camera never pans round to see Judy Murray looking to the sky exasperated, or shaking her head. Or pointing and swearing at Andy's opponent or the umpire. So if she can do this when a player who _is_ expected to perform flawlessly makes a mistake or has a hard time, anyone can!

Inwardly there may well have been times when she was thinking, "Awful shot son" or "Wrong choice Andy", but, outwardly what you see is support for the next point. Doesn't that say it all?

Coping with and reviewing a loss

Tennis can be an expensive sport to fund, especially when you move up grades of tournaments and you have to travel the length and breadth of Britain. But it is your decision to support your child, to spend your money on the development of your tennis prodigy, and yes, sometimes your child doesn't play well and has a bad day. That is life.

A parent needs to stay supportive when their child comes off court crying or disappointed – this outburst of emotion shows they care. If your child is not too bothered about their loss / poor performance, maybe they don't want it as much as you feel they should do, and it might be time to reassess what direction their tennis goes.

Sometimes tennis players need space when they lose. Avoid forcing your child to talk with you immediately after a loss. Don't relive the match blow by blow, they are already doing that inside their own head. You won't help by doing it for them right now.

So change the topic of conversation, lighten the mood. Go for dinner or watch a film. Learn to always leave the tennis on the court. Make your child feel valuable and reinforce his / her self-esteem, especially when he / she loses and emphasise that, win or lose, you love them just the same. Remind them what Rafa Nadal says: that he is no better or worse a person after a win or a loss, he is the same person.

By all means the next day sit down and rationally go through the match / tournament. Always start with what worked and went well for your child, as juniors have a habit of over-exaggerating just how bad they played.

Often you will hear, "I was rubbish, everything was rubbish, nothing worked". So it is important to debrief constructively:

- Wait until the time is right – the next day when your child has calmed down perhaps;

- Ask them what they thought went well and also what went wrong, and offer your own opinions in a calm manner. Offer positive solutions for the child to work on – so he / she can take responsibility for their own actions and recognise that making a mistake is a learning process rather than the end of the world;

- Be assertive but not overbearing – there's a fine line between encouragement and a telling off!

- Finally, but importantly, try to 'sandwich' your criticism between a couple of compliments – ensuring your child starts and finishes the conversation in a good place emotionally.

Remember: It is important to let your child take responsibility for their success or failure and to face up to what happened, good or bad, and help them avoid making excuses. But it's OK to help them along the way with some positive support, as outlined above.

<u>Sportsmanship</u>

The next part of this section addresses how best to deal with something that has quite likely occurred on a regular basis in your own household – but something that should have no place on a tennis court, namely: temper tantrums. What should you do if your child is throwing a wobbler on court? How do you deal with it if your child is shouting (or swearing), throwing their racket, getting upset or even blatantly cheating with bad line calls – basically, losing control?

Unfortunately, like in all sports, junior sportsmen and women want to copy and replicate what their sporting heroes and those they look up to do. Footballers spit, shout at the referee and dive in the penalty area. Rugby players throw sly punches when the official's back is turned. Tennis is no different. We see, on occasions, bad behaviour by the professional players on court – the Djokovic racket smash is a pertinent example nowadays – though many of us will think further back to the infamous words and (reverse) inspiration for this book: "You cannot be serious"!

Often, this kind of behaviour goes unpunished. Furthermore, it generally does not lead to an improved performance, but what it does do is show junior players behaviour that they then think is acceptable or 'cool' to do when playing. If you are having such problems with your child, I can recommend a few solutions.   Just to clarify, I am referring to serious behaviour issues here. I am not talking about an outburst of frustration or emotion – I am talking about a total breakdown on court. Try one method before moving onto the next, as each step is more drastic.

- Sit down with your child and reason with them. Explain that getting angry and annoyed does not help them play any better. You could also give them specific examples of how this behaviour has never been productive for them in the past.

- If that doesn't work, the next step is to film them (if possible on your phone) if you see it happening and afterwards, play it back to them. Show them how they look and hopefully it will make them realise how they appear silly and cause slight embarrassment. Hopefully you can both laugh at it, but the child will have made a mental note that really, it is not a laughing matter if they take their tennis seriously.

- If over time you are seeing an improvement in your child's behaviour, keep working with them to make them understand their behaviour is not helping their play and overall results, and hopefully their behaviour will improve over a period of time.

- If filming still fails to get the message across, and you are seeing no marked improvement, you have a couple of choices. Either take them out of all competitions or explain to your child that if their behaviour on court persists, you will take them off the court regardless of the score. This is your last resort: calmly walk on court and, whether your child is winning or losing, rationally explain you will not put up with this behaviour and remove them, regardless of the score or stage in the match.

This seems harsh I know. And it is far from ideal. But your child has been warned and what you are trying to do is break a habit. You may find doing this once is enough, or you may find you need to carry out with your threat several times for your child to get the message but this is a good habit to break at a young age.

These suggestions might be hard to accept and carry out. But it is always good practice to have clear boundaries for behaviour you will and will not accept. I'm quite sure you have rules that govern your child's behaviour elsewhere – at home, at school, when visiting friends / family – and on the court is no different.

Before moving on, I will tell you one of many experiences I have had with a young player who demonstrated very challenging behaviour on court. It happened with a boy about eight years of age, and was during a tournament I was running several years ago. It was the height of the summer, about 30 degrees Celsius (Yes, even in Scotland), and all tennis courts were being used for various matches with dozens of people watching – enjoying their ice creams and cold drinks.

This eight-year-old (let's call him 'Tom') had a match with a slightly older boy, who was a better player, and his parents were watching like many others. The match started and it didn't take long before Tom started to get upset. He was losing and was throwing his racket into the back fence. Not long after came the tears and shouting out, and he threw in a few dishonest line calls as well. I am sure you can picture the scene.

Tom's opponent understood the younger child's torment and was trying to give Tom some points – but it was clear he was starting to feel very uncomfortable. I approached Tom's mother and asked if she was going to deal with the situation. All I got back was: "But it's character building".

I was eventually forced to tell her if she didn't deal with him I would. She reluctantly took him off the court crying and, by this stage, shouting at his Mum.

Now fast forward about six years to the same 'Tom', now in his early teens. I was coaching and popped to the courts to watch one of my players. On the next court, Tom was playing against a decent player, and was in a close match.

Again, there was a good crowd watching including his Dad and again Tom was shouting out in a temper, not only to himself but to his Dad, as well as making some dubious line calls. The Dad approached me and asked what could be done and I gave him a pretty honest answer. But all along I was thinking it had taken six years to address the situation, by which time it was going to be very hard to break his behaviour as it had been allowed to continue for so long.

His parents obviously presumed his attitude would change when he grew up. Unfortunately, with the emotional fragility and mood swings that come hand-in-hand with adolescence, it actually exaggerated the problems even more. As mentioned earlier, Albert Einstein once said, "The sign of insanity is doing the same thing over and over again and expecting a different outcome". It was a long shot that his behaviour was going to correct itself without any help.

I would like to conclude this section, and the book, by using an example of Roger Federer in his younger days. Federer is the greatest tennis player the world has ever seen. So it may be surprising to learn how, at one point, he was far from the model tennis player with unshakable emotional control he is today. But, with the right support and coaching, Federer – once tagged as the 'Little Satan' by a coach – managed to gain control over his issues. The following extract is taken from a Roger Federer biography.

"His performance already showed signs of genius. But controlling his temper was the biggest problem that would afflict him throughout his childhood. He was often out of control on the court. He lost his temper after hitting dumb shots and rarely went through a day without hurling his racket against the fence. [His parents] Robert and Lynette were embarrassed when they saw their son's behaviour during tournaments. Roger could not understand this. He was never offensive to umpires, linesmen or opposing players. His anger was reserved for himself.

"From the age of 10 to 14, Roger spent more time with his coach than his own parents. Coach Carter taught him flawless technique on his ground strokes and serves and watched him grow into his body and start dominating opponents. Carter and Roger spent countless hours discussing the mental side of the game, not just strategy and psychology, but also about the importance of being gracious, polite and reigning in your emotions."

The greatest player – and the greatest example.

Final Thoughts

By taking charge of your game, no matter how old you are, no matter how good your skill level is, it will give you a sense of going out to win a match rather than going out not to lose.

Taking responsibility for everything you do in your tennis match can also certainly help if you take the ACE approach into other areas of your life. Staying in control of your emotions will stand you in good stead in any environment.

There are no big secrets to winning. Achieving positive results has little to do with superior intelligence or special skills beyond sound core-abilities. If the world's top players were so superior to the rest of the professionals on their circuit, why do they still lose to these players on occasion, as Federer, Nadal, Williams and Sharapova did at Wimbledon 2013?

The difference between success and failure in competition is remarkably small, and often it is down to the psychological condition of players that makes the difference. Using the simple habits and techniques outlined in this book will help you achieve that mental edge. By having an understanding of what is happening in the present, and taking clear and decisive action, with a clear head, to deal with what is happening, you will see marked improvement in your performance, and most likely your results too.

The tools and tips are spread across the whole of this book, but it will be your desire for change, your desire to actually see how good you can become, and your motivation to do something about it that will ultimately determine how proficient your tennis game becomes, and subsequently how much enjoyment and pleasure you will allow yourself to experience.

I wish you all the best in your future, within tennis and life, and hope I have given you a brief and manageable understanding of how you can move your game up to the next level.

To find fulfilment in your tennis, it must first be fun. And, even though your tennis should always be fun, remember... You CAN be serious, too.